Deliver Us *from* Meltdowns

And Other Real-World Prayers *for* Parents

JANEL BREITENSTEIN

AMEN

AMEN Editions, an imprint of Andrews McMeel Publishing
a division of Andrews McMeel Universal
1130 Walnut Street, Kansas City, Missouri 64106

ameneditions.com

25 26 27 28 29 RLP 10 9 8 7 6 5 4 3 2 1

ISBN: 979-8-8816-0236-9

Library of Congress Control Number: 2025931927

Editor: Jennifer Leight
Designer: Noora Cox
Production Manager: Tamara Haus

Cover image used under license from Shutterstock

FSC www.fsc.org
MIX
Paper | Supporting responsible forestry
FSC® C102842

AMEN Editions is committed to the responsible use of natural resources and is dedicated to understanding, measuring, and reducing the impact of our products on the natural world. By choosing this product, you are supporting responsible management of the world's forests. The FSC® label means that the materials used for this product come from well-managed FSC®-certified forests, recycled materials, and other controlled sources.

ATTENTION: SCHOOLS AND BUSINESSES
AMEN Editions books are available at quantity discounts with bulk purchase for educational, business, or sales promotional use. For information, please email the AMEN Editions Special Sales Department: sales@ameneditions.com.

To all those who prayed for me—
but especially Dad and Mom,
who knew and lived that knowing,
following, and depending on Jesus
is always infinitely worth it

♥

Contents

Introduction

Parenting has a way of bringing us to our knees, doesn't it?

One moment you're googling "how to get poop out of the bathtub"; the next, tiny arms loop around your neck, your heart suddenly a puddle. Parenting is a wild, nonstop mix of messy and marvelous, exhausting and exhilarating. Maybe, like me, you've discovered prayer isn't just a helpful option—it's often the *only* one.

My husband and I discovered just how very far this parenting thing was beyond our control even before our first child was born. From a layoff at seven months pregnant, to a car accident at thirty-seven weeks, to the demise of a generously named "birth plan," prayer became our own umbilical cord. Prayer tethered us to a God extending truth, compassion, stamina, and presence when we couldn't have found them with a night-light.

And the pandemonium didn't stop there. At one point, I was hauling around four kids under four. Wet wipes and soggy-cornered board books wallpapered my days. Through all those dimpled hands tugging me awake and endless loops of diapers and dishes, I've learned prayer isn't just about answers. It's connecting with our God-with-Us in parenting moments from desperate to ridiculous. After all, this God—who chose to enter our chaos in His own diapers—knows exactly what it's like to nurture wayward, wiggly kids.

Perhaps you're reading while rocking a baby refusing sleep, wrangling a defiant toddler, or waiting up for a teenager who views curfew as a suggestion. Or maybe you've been blindsided by tough questions, checkout-line tantrums, or the eternal mystery of why kids perceive toothbrushing as cruel and unusual punishment. Wherever you are, this book is for you.

These prayers emerge from the something-might-be-on-fire of real-life parenting. I've prayed through it all: sibling squabbles, potty-training catastrophes, teenage heartbreaks, and even a cancer scare with my son. I've prayed hiding in the pantry for seven seconds of silence and while scrubbing dried mac and cheese off the walls. Sometimes those prayers were eloquent, sometimes wordless, sometimes as simple as "Help."

No matter what words (or groans) you bring, God hears you. When you can't patch together a coherent sentence, He's there, laboring invisibly—as parents do—behind the scenes. He carried His kids, Israel, through the wilderness "as a father carries his child," and lends a hand through where's-my-backpack morning mayhem to midnight feedings.

He witnesses every sacrifice, every fatigued sigh, every whispered "I'm sorry" after you lost your patience (again). And He's active in and for your kids—knitting their cells together in the womb, marveling over their discoveries, holding them in loss, and steering them through every stage. He's present for them. He's present for *you*.

To dig deeper into God's character and His promises, check out the Scriptures referenced in margin notes throughout.

Whether I was pretending to camp in the jungle of the steamy bathroom with a coughing toddler or stumbling into a child's room at 3 a.m., God has received me, enveloped me. He's held my shaking hands, wiped relentless tears, and quietly reiterated that I'm never alone. God could easily recite my sensational top-five (okay, fifteen) parenting crash and burns, and ration a box of tissues over the highlight reel.

And in those day-in, day-out moments, He alters us—if we're open to the two-way conversation. The more I talk with *and listen to* God, the more He transforms me to look like my heavenly Dad: wiser, more patient, more forgiving, and (on good days) more selfless, more willing to trust His ideas over mine. For all prayer does for me, it's primarily my avenue to simply be *with* God.

He's parented His fair share of rebels, prodigals, and the equivalent of kids who baptize the cat in the backyard. And yet He moves toward us, over and over, with undeserved kindness. He nourishes us daily. Carries us. Washes us. Clothes us. Creates with us. Sings over us. Bandages our owies, internal and external. Chats with us. Gives tailor-made gifts. Delights in growing us up.

Genesis 12:1–2; Psalm 28:9, 103:2–3, 147:3; Zephaniah 3:17; Matthew 6:28–33, 7:9–11; 1 Peter 2:24; 2 Peter 3

My hope is that in these pages and intimate moments you'll find not just words for your godward pleas and much-needed humor for the parenting roller coaster but also the One riding alongside. He's engineering every part of the ride, even when you wish you could get off, or you're pretty sure you were too short or terrified in the first place.

May His adventure catapult you to never-imagined heights—and reinforce that both you and your rowdy, much-adored kids are deeply loved.

Ask, seek, knock—

Janel

Prayers *for* Peace & Patience

Deliver Us *from* Meltdowns

Tamer of Tempests,

I know You didn't miss the storm my child just unleashed—those arrowed eyebrows, the dramatic gestures, that thundering voice. How can I sell this kid on Your promise of "blessed are the peacemakers" . . . and trust it myself?

I need you, Prince of Peace, Wonderful Counselor. Every day, of course. But especially after that F5 temper-tornado from my little ray of sunshine here. I'm not sure I was very calm either. Even if my conscience is (mostly) clear, that doesn't mean I don't have room to grow to be more like You. *1 Corinthians 4:4*

My emotional flares currently include anger, maybe even fear, embarrassment, discouragement, exhaustion, powerlessness. But You already know that. *Psalm 139:1–4*

You witnessed what I said or didn't. You saw how the moment tempted me to lash out, hide behind snark, or maybe just shut down.

Help me sense when and how to lean into wise, measured parental firmness . . . even in the middle of a pint-sized meltdown. I need Your know-how to bring more of Your character into my parenting, following Your Spirit and showing Your fruit—especially patience and self-control—even when I'd rather duck and cover or just show this kid who's boss. Show me the time and place for righteous anger that brings about Your purposes and carefully removes sin and injustice, not selfish *Galatians 5:22–23* outbursts that seek our own purposes like a force of nature. Empower our family to be, like You, quick to listen, slow to speak, slow to anger.

James 1:19–20

I ask for wisdom to figure out what just blew through that interaction—like just what my child was protecting that felt precious in the moment. What our individual contributions were (helping us each own up to 100 percent of ours). What parts of this tiny or teenage tempest might have been from You, and which You'd never take credit for. What needs to be overlooked. What must be forgiven like You forgive us.

James 1:5, Matthew 7:3–5, Proverbs 19:11, Mark 11:25

Because, ultimately, we want to seek peace, understanding, and love but not gloss over what could (or even should) change. It's how You approached conflict with us (aka the Gospel).[1] You told the whole truth about what wasn't working with our ways and within our hearts. Then You held nothing back to close the gap between us. You restored us to better than before.

2 Corinthians 5:18–20

With You as our guide, we can rebuild like this in our relationships, too. (Right?)

So help me crave true peace as much as You do, even when it lies on the other side of conflict. I want to make peace. Not fake it. Not break it.[2] Shape a culture in this messy, beautiful family of both "I'm sorry" and "I forgive you." Start with me as I go back to lead the disaster-recovery effort.

Matthew 5:9

amen.

Help Me Pick My Battles *(and Find the Spoons)*

To Our Peacemaker,

Whether it's screen time, the state of this child's hazmat-level bedroom, what they're wearing to school, when to do homework—I appreciate the reminder there's compromise to be had (on my child's side, right?).

Regarding the room: Considering the dozen pair of scissors and five open boxes of cereal under this kid's bed, I would at least ask they return all the spoons.

Still—You approach me not as merely a servant to be governed but as a person in Your image. Help me extend that kind of dignity, even when faced with this child's (impressively witty) snark or competition-worthy eye-rolling. Show me how to draw the line on the respect I must teach, while demonstrating respect in return. This may require Your help to suppress my sass.

Ephesians 6:2–3

Don't tell my kids, but sometimes I'm less flexible than I could be . . . because I'm so exhausted. Or what they want is so stinkin' inconvenient. Or I'm afraid of appearances. Or it's just not the proper way (mashed potatoes aren't paint!). But I guess I could let them wear kid underwear backward so they can see the picture. (Something tells me they'll get it on the right way someday.)

You reach toward us, offering dignity and an ear to our desires—and yet managing to forbid, reorder, and reform desires that hurt us.

Psalm 38:9–10, 89:46; Proverbs 13:12; Ezekiel 36:26; Romans 12:2

Self-discipline is so often learned by discipline applied to us. Does that mean I'm off the hook with the request for only fruit snacks and barbecue potato chips for lunch?

You want Your people to consider others more than themselves. So I'm guessing sometimes I model this by bending toward my child, and other times shape that kind of character in them. Maybe it would actually celebrate childhood a little if this kid wore fairy wings to the doctor's office. Philippians 2:3–4

But I do know entitlement looks tacky on pretty much everyone. This world doesn't need any more divas.

I see You responding to Abraham's plea with compromise. (Tell the truth: Would You have bargained if it were about curfew?) You beg us, "Come now, let us reason together." And You remind me that wisdom that comes from You is both *peaceable* and *reasonable*. So maybe I *don't* allow them to start a campfire in the yard, but I *do* help set up a tent in the living room? Genesis 18:16–33 Isaiah 1:18 James 3:17

Yet You're pretty clear on what *not* to compromise on—Your ways. We want to love You with everything. Matthew 22:37–39

Would that include building a life-sized castle of marshmallows? Inquiring minds want to know.

Amen.

Hold My Tongue *in the* Face *of* Unsolicited Advice

To the One Whose Word Is Perfect,

Whether it's sleep scheduling, discipline, or nutrition, everyone from in-laws to complete strangers is a fount of knowledge I didn't necessarily ask for. Maybe they're even speaking harshly to my child, or failing to truly see them.

It's a loop of "You should try . . .", "When I had my kids, I made sure to . . .", "I wouldn't let that child . . .", and "Is that really what you want to do?"

What if some hairy little part of me—which should be living under a bridge and demanding riddles to cross—wants to tell someone to put a sock in it?

All those "shoulds" can dig their tiny claws into my brain at 3:00 a.m., making me second-guess (and third- and fourth-guess) whether I know what I'm doing at all. Then I start replaying that reel of moments that would cause anyone in their right mind to question whether my offspring were raised by wolves.

♡ Psalm 4:7

I do want to be teachable. I do. You remind me that only idiots despise wisdom; You say wisdom's better than cold, hard cash.

Proverbs 1:7, 16:16

And Your followers are quick to listen, slow to speak, slow to anger. (Is it bad if I'd like more people to heed the whole "slow to speak" bit?)

James 1:19

I do ask for other voices in my kids' lives, and the rich benefits of community: people invested in them, abundant in areas where I'm sorely lacking, and (ahem) intimately involved enough to speak into my kids' lives.

I admit the "time to keep silence, and a time to speak" thing is tough to master. So tamp down my ego, if You would, and help me extract any percentage that is in fact worth listening to from that little advice column so freely given in the freezer aisle. Lend me insights (not assumptions) into the giver's heart—whether it's a desire to keep others from making their mistakes, to protect, to be superior. . . .

Ecclesiastes 3:7

But help me respond graciously, like Jesus did, to whatever's insulting. Let me overlook an offense.

Luke 6:26–27, 1 Peter 3:9, 1 Corinthians 4:12

Proverbs 19:11

Still—You made me this kid's parent on purpose. If I were just pleasing people, I wouldn't be serving You. So please give me wisdom and courage to confidently follow You rather than be jerked around by all the bright ideas of all the people who don't know and truly love my child.

Galatians 1:10

Sure, silence is golden on my part. But handing out duct tape is a tempting silver. Might want to hide it from me next time.

amen.

For the Passing *of the* Potty Hours

Good Father,

Maybe I've never prayed this much for poop. Never talked about it this much with other adults. (You know you're a real parent when it gets in your eyebrow.) But here we all are.

I'm thankful my child's digestive system functions properly, most of the time, and that they *can* be potty trained, fun as this is. Many parents and children around the world don't enjoy that privilege.

1 Corinthians 12:22, 23

I acknowledge Your goodness in making my child's body: that though some body parts are far more presentable than others, every part is indispensable—and engineered perfectly by You, without shame. Right now, I'm here . . . waiting . . . for the sake of teaching my child their next step in self-mastery, and eventually self-care.

In Your wisdom, You stitched our souls to these bodies. We're born needing and longing to be loved and nurtured not only at our best, but in our nakedness. Our most vulnerable parts call for the most tender care.

John 1:14, Philippians 2:7

No doubt someone potty trained Your Son's own wiggly body that would rather go out and play already. Thank You for wrapping Yourself so personally in our need and liability. For dignifying these bodies. For becoming someone who'd require this intimate level of care to thrive. In so many ways, Your body was given for us. To us.

Luke 22:19

So here I am, carpet cleaner, TP, and child-sized rewards on standby. I can think of plenty more efficient ways to spend my hours—yet love slows me down once more, interrupting my productivity. It extends me a free coupon for more connection with this little person who's thrilled far more by time with me than by folded laundry or answered texts. You so often embodied that holy interruptibility—whether by a bleeding woman or a rich young ruler. *Mark 5:25–34, 10:17–22*

So for just a moment, derail my steaming, chuffing train of thought and my to-do list. Help me take that beat to read a chewed-up board book, or to celebrate when something lands at last beneath my child. Grant me patience and kindness with the next accident. Teach me to love my child sincerely. *Romans 12:9* Guide me toward Your rare gift of presence, even as I kneel next to the potty. Transform this very human, mundane moment into an opportunity for us to love each other.

And if You could move things along? Even better.

amen.

Grant Me Infinite Patience *for* Endless Whys

God Who Hears Us,

You've heard it: Sometimes for my kids, I might as well be named Siri, or Alexa.

When were olives invented? Does W start with D? What's the longest anyone's ever Hula-Hooped? How do babies get in stomachs?

Maybe the questions bubble up at bedtime. Or when we're just trying to get out the door without someone pooping their pants. At that point, I'm not really in the can-we-grow-hot-dogs-in-the-garden headspace.

But the questions get harder. Not only is it possible I forgot how to complete fifth-grade math; I also need to answer why a friend got cancer. Or why someone had a miscarriage. Or how we know the Bible is true.

Guess kids aren't the only ones with bottomless questions. (Can I request bottomless chips and salsa instead?)

Thank You for how, from the Psalms to the Gospels, You grant dignity to questions and searching and curiosity. You bend toward Thomas, John the Baptist, Elijah, Zacchaeus, Mary, Martha. You walk alongside pain-twisted disciples on the road to Emmaus. *Luke 24:13–35*

You love seekers. *Matthew 7:8* You named Your people after a man who wrestled with You. *Genesis 32:28*

You could've created a horde of robots to worship as You deserve. But You shaped brains, allowing creative thought and wonder and what-if. Like Your own mind.

You hunger for real, not blind, intimacy with us. You long to be known, wooing us to feel our way toward You. Your creation screams this.

Psalm 19:1–4, Acts 17:26–27, Romans 1:19–20

So empower me to offer dignity, patience, and space for "how-big-is-the-universe" and "how-many-bugs-are-in-the-world" questions. Let me feed rather than quench their thirst to know and understand.

Share discernment for the "question beneath the question" that my kids' hearts are really asking. And humility when I don't know, plus diligence to seek answers.

For life's unanswerables, steer us both to realize the otherness of Your thoughts and ways—which make You all the more worthy of worship.

Deuteronomy 29:29, Isaiah 55:8–9

Increase our trust in the gap between our understanding and Yours. Comfort us that we need not abandon peace until all questions are answered.

*Proverbs 3:5–6**

Especially when Grandma doesn't quite know how to respond when asked if the world was black and white when she was a kid.

amen.

Peace Be *with* You, *and* Also *with* Your Siblings

To the Triune God Who Is One,

Ephesians 6:17

Between the flying insults, snacks "accidentally" chucked at a sibling, and victims wailing as if their pet guinea pig were lost to the struggle, I need that helmet of salvation. Maybe equipped with earplugs. (Oh, and a referee's jersey and whistle, maybe with a roll of duct tape?)

We do love each other. But in this moment we may not like each other. And surely every human relationship tumbles through seasons where affection wanes and irritation swells.

1 Corinthians 13:5

But real love, Your brand of love, isn't touchy, rude, grudge-holding, or demanding. It's easy to love when everyone else is angelic. It's much harder when they're mocking your haircut, pounding on the bathroom door, crashing down carefully constructed block creations like a T. rex, or acting just plain grumpy.

Isaiah 53:6, Romans 5:6, 8

Yet that's also where love is tested to see if it's really like Yours. Because You loved us when we were pitted against You—for way more than dropping Your toothbrush in the toilet.

I would love silence and harmony. Though I confess I'm tempted to bypass that whole conflict-management-skills-for-a-lifetime thing and opt for these little minions just cleaning the house (beginning in separate rooms, of course).

Replace any passivity in me with intentionality. Exhaustion with holy, grace-filled stamina. And my own annoyance and short fuse with the patience of Job. Grant me wisdom, discernment, and smart questions to carry out thoughtful justice in my own home.

Help each one of us take off anger, verbal venom, and disdain—as fast and completely as a snowsuit when we've gotta use the bathroom. Teach me to cultivate and instill the makings of true peace in these humans: confession, forgiveness, compassion, humility, kindness, and a long fuse with each other's squirreliness and offense.

Colossians 3:8

Colossians 3:12

These are the virtues that flip the world upside down when others might opt for revenge, outrage, attacks, and/or cage fighting. Thank You for loving us and bearing with us even when we're being juvenile. Let us be a family that reaches toward each other.

And not just to pull each other's hair.

amen.

Guide Us *Through the* Carpool Chaos Line

Shepherd,

Here it is: the daily rainbow of backpacks and lunch boxes and expressions—experiences, really—gushing from the school doors as if they can't vacate fast enough. Please keep each child safe as I search for one or more faces that matter the most to me.

Those kids will scramble into this car, pulling the chaos out there into this vehicle and vaporizing my last few minutes of quiet.

Thank You for walking with them this whole day when I cannot. You've witnessed, and offered Your presence in, their wins and losses, triumphs and misdeeds, rejection and acceptance, thoughts and actions of beauty and cruelty both given and received. You know what they will reveal and conceal in the walls of this vehicle.

Help me to be a trustworthy recipient—whatever version of them plops into the seat, from hangry to happy. Even when I receive the dregs of my child's day.

I'm grateful for the abundant education opportunities for my child's mind. Yet I acknowledge they're being discipled, too, throughout the day by their experiences.

Thank You for this daily rhythm allowing us presence with each other, the time and space to reflect and connect.

You ask me to keep Your commands on my heart, and teach my kids diligently; to talk about them when we sit or travel together. I'd guess this vehicle qualifies. Help me know how to tenderly, intentionally lay Your ways and words over this child's day and heart. Let me gently tip their chins up to see Your presence with them always.

Deuteronomy 6:7

Ephesians 4:29

Psalm 139:7–10

I want to receive my child as You receive me. Would You silence distractions inside and outside my head? (Even the not-so-gentle words attempting to sneak out as I navigate traffic!) Let my child see Your welcome, Your smile, Your embrace through me. You lend me both ear and empathy. Shape me into a parent who listens—and whose kids want to talk to them.

Romans 15:7

James 1:19

I ask You for discernment to look beyond how my kids say something to what they're trying to communicate, courage to pursue what I should, self-control to overlook what I should and not leap into judgment, wisdom to form both right responses and questions to ask, and playfulness to enter into my child's world like You did into ours. Remind me what I don't know—and what it's like to be a kid.

This carpool line may mean chaos—but for what's about to descend here, it's my cherished chaos. Bring it on.

Amen.

Though We Walk *Through the Valley of* Friend Drama

Great Mediator,

These kids aren't getting along. Could be the problem is their kid, mine, or both. Once again I'm in the weird spot of wondering whether I barge in tweeting my referee whistle or just coach from the sidelines.

Either way, in a culture where outrage is the new black, this is our little corner of the world to change. Spats like these are just the right calisthenics for weightier conflicts in this kid's future.

So allow me to really listen to this child—and if I have opportunity, the other one, too.

Psalm 128:1, Matthew 6:10

Show me how to raise neither doormats nor bullies but kids who care about Your Word and ways here. Teach us to navigate setting healthy boundaries, overlooking offense, returning kindness for rudeness, getting help, or talking out the issues. Even when the other kid is acting like a toad. *Oops.* Prevent us from labeling and name-calling.

Proverbs 19:11, 1 Peter 3:9

Psalm 37:8

Let us "refrain from anger, and forsake wrath." Nothing good's gonna happen if this isn't about Your Kingdom. Anger could catalyze more of what's bad. Though part of me would like to yank at least one of these kids by the ear and shout something super-productive, like "Don't be a turd!"

James 1:20

So help me, rather than just coming out swinging on my child's behalf, to ask thoughtful, heart-level questions to determine my child's contribution(s), even if I perceive their portion is teeny-tiny. Let the two of us set the tone for genuine apology and requests for forgiveness: for building a relational bridge, like You did.

Matthew 7:5

Ephesians 2:14

When it comes to anger, we all assume we're like You, flipping over temple tables. If our kid's "in the right," we feel justified . . . even if it starts mattering more than the other person.[3]

Galatians 5:22

Please grant both my child and me Your Spirit's self-control and deep love for the other person. Remind us who You say my child is, and how secure we are with You as Judge and Defender. Unhitch our God-given value from who others think or say we are, and our ability to be superior.

Truth: This kid could "win" here and lose everything that matters. Because loving each other is how people see You. It's where the rubber meets the road on whether You're really living in us.

Psalm 133:1, 1 John 4:12

Remind us how much we've been forgiven. Especially when I feel the urge to tell that other . . . *child of God* exactly what I think.

Amen.

He Who *Is* Free *from the* Grumps *Is* Free Indeed

Great Harmonizer,

If I were You, I might want to steer clear of this place today. (But please don't!) Ain't nobody happy around here. We apparently all barreled out of the wrong side of the bed this morning.

And when one mixes a bunch of relatives with bad moods, it's not like that negative-times-a-negative-equals-a-positive thing. It's more like "negative to the *n*th degree." In other words, watch out.

All those fruits of the spirit—love, joy, peace, patience, etcetera? Let's just say that today, they're showing up more like raisins smooshed and forgotten under the car seat cushion. And with these kids nitpicking at each other, I have fantasized about spiriting away to someplace beachy and so wonderfully silent, tiny umbrellas stuck in the drinks.

Psalm 133:1 You love it when siblings dwell in unity. So I'm asking for supernatural intervention here. It's really the only antidote to our snarling, oversensitivity, and good old-fashioned snippiness. *Romans 12:10* Let us outdo each other in showing honor rather than annoyance.

Show us, please, how to "put on . . . compassionate hearts, kindness, humility, meekness, and patience, bearing with one another and, if one has a complaint against another, forgiving each other; as the Lord has forgiven you, so you also must forgive. And above all these put on love, which binds everything together in perfect harmony." (You said it, which must mean it's possible in this household?) Colossians 3:12–14

Help me discern when to simply separate everyone until the storm passes—or when to stick out the conflict management, though I would rather be having a root canal. Remind us what we like about each other, and why.

I echo the ancient request to make me an instrument of Your peace here at this squalling little address, planting seeds of love and forgiveness in place of irritation and injury.[4] Even when my child stomps on my toes; complains about dinner, chores, and our brand of toilet paper; and rolls their eyes hard enough to be audible, empower me to respond with graciousness and appropriate boundaries.

You're slow to anger and abounding in love even on the days when tripping over a backpack might as well be a land mine. Certainly You can keep me calm and navigate us through a bad case of the crabbies. Psalm 103:8

Could noise-canceling headphones be part of that path to holiness?

Amen.

Lord, Make *Us* Losers

Director of Our Paths,

Whether my kid gets saddled with the dud card in the deck or doesn't get picked for the team, losing—and even failure—is a part of life. And it's a good thing.

If this kid never encountered anything tough or something they can't do, we'd be looking at character with the lifting power of cherry gelatin. They'd lack the resilience to shake off the puddle on the way to the school bus. They'd have the courage of Chicken Little.

Thankfully, this kid's value doesn't lie in their ability to be the best or to be comfortable in their little world without mosquitoes or hangnails.

So make us losers. Wait! Make us *good* losers. Make us people who can return to joy—to well-being anchored in You, no matter what. After all, they'll need resilience if someday I get to smoke this kid at strategy games.

In Your wisdom, questions bubble to the surface when things don't go our way. Maybe they start with, *How do I deal? Does not getting what I want = No one loves me?* And as we age, maybe, *What does this say about me?* Or, *Why didn't God do what I wanted? (Did He hear? Is He here?)* Or maybe, *What do I do now?*

*Luke 22:42 But even Jesus didn't always get a yes. And when I think of the Saturday after He died, I know sometimes what looks like smashing failure is ultimately stunning victory. In fact, it's far better than before.

In light of eternity and *Your* priorities, help us give appropriate weight to both success and failure here on the third rock. After all, even achieving our own goals and dreams, without You, will only leave us empty. Somehow achieving the highest bowling score—or even the highest grades—just wasn't meant to satisfy.

Jeremiah 2:13

So don't let me stack the deck, making sure this kid never leaves their personal, far-too-tiny-and-comfortable vision of happiness and perfection. Don't let me stand in the way of holy grit, and the greatness You've inlaid.

From the kid upending the game board to the one stomping off the baseball field, grant us the gift of perspective and patience amid every crash and burn. You have this way of making beautiful things out of dust. And even what people intend for evil, You intend for good.

Genesis 50:20

Still, let me appropriately receive this child's sadness like You would, with the right amount of lament. (Maybe not a sob session over losing a round of dominoes?) I don't want to just metaphorically slap on a superhero bandage. You remind me that mourning—sharing in Your sadness about what's not right—is a place of blessing, because You've got comfort in store. Even in loss, point the way to gratitude.

Matthew 5:4

We might need a map. Or a nap.

amen.

Give Us *This* Day *Our* Humble Pie

Great High Priest,

Hallelujah that a good parent doesn't equal a perfect parent. 'Cause just now I blew it.

I should mention I'm grateful for the highly uncomfortable mercy of Your pointing out my sin rather than leaving me in my slop. The person whom You set free really *is* free.

John 8:36

But this is . . . an opportunity. (Trust me, I'm not patting myself on the back.) I'd rather model genuine confession and repentance for this kid than polish my own halo, floating around on a pink cloud of my self-righteousness. Please show our whole family how to voluntarily chuck sin's blindfold.

What still lies within my power: those earth-shattering little words. *I'm sorry.*

Because to be human is to break stuff. To screw up, taking those we love with us. You know and I know that sometimes I tear down the house I'm trying to build with my own two hands. Perfection is Yours, not mine.

Romans 3:23, 1 John 1:8

Proverbs 14:7

Prevent me from forfeiting my ability to change, by lying/denying/blaming. Including but not limited to mouthy children, left-out toys piercing the ball of my foot, abbreviated REM cycles related to parenthood, overfilled-and-spilled glasses of grape juice on optimistically purchased white furniture.

And lest I shove it aside, in the future, help me intentionally do a 180.

So I'm agreeing with You that I was wrong. Please forgive me. I welcome it.

My love for You grows (as You intend) the more I realize how much I'm forgiven. As I ask forgiveness from my child, and mean it, show me how to reconcile our relationship and restore what's been lost. Would You—as long as it's right to You—protect and heal my kids from my sin's fallout?

Luke 7:47

(I would also welcome some help in the self-compassion department, trusting in Your mercy.)

1 John 1:9, 2 Corinthians 7:10

Let this family become fluent in a heartfelt "I'm sorry/I forgive you" language and culture. Teach me how to take responsibility for both the attitude of my heart and the tangible wrongdoing that came out of it. This may or may not require the spiritual equivalent of a FEMA truck.

The more I get honest about my sin and failure, the more Your Gospel shows itself as real in this house. And just maybe, it's more likely to draw in my child. So rather than my perceived flawlessness (as a total poseur) taking center stage, let it be Yours. These kids need You a lot more than a pseudo-perfect parent.

amen.

Be *My* Hiding Place—*Literally*

Prince of Peace,

I just. Need. A moment. Alone. Pleaseohplease.

Fingers curling under the bathroom door. Endless choruses calling me. All the things that used to be mine—bed, body, space to think thoughts higher than sippy cup thoughts or screen time negotiations, space to poop in solitude—are now up for grabs.

Psalm 23:1–2

You've promised me still waters, green pastures. Is it selfish to request those could just be . . . all mine? Help me recognize and accept them.

Empower me to ask for the help I need from others, and to set appropriate boundaries with these little people so I'm at least not overfunctioning. Pretty sure these kids should pick up their own socks.

Pull me into peace, physical or otherwise, and teach me how to find it. Make me an instrument of Your peace here.

There's no guarantee this madhouse is going to settle down anytime soon. But I trust it's just like that night with Your disciples, when peace meant more than zero wind or waves: It was the One they had in their boat.

Pass the motion-sickness tabs, please.

Amen.

Prayers *for* Trust & Surrender

Get Behind Me, *Helicopter Parent*

All-Powerful One,

Any way my kids could thrive in a sanitized rubber room?

You've charged me with both protecting my kids and training them to build enough strength for the complexities and demands of adulthood. Oy vey.

There's so much to monitor: initially, the veggies eaten, every tiny tooth brushed, making sure no one gets clobbered on the swing set. Later it's the grades, screens, friends, clothing that at least approaches appropriate.

Where's that sweet spot between "no one left me unprotected; my parent set smart boundaries" and "I'm resilient for every hurdle of adult life; no one snowplowed my obstacles"? Between kids weak and hurt, and kids strong for a lifetime?

Your boundaries, from Sabbath to sex, are good. Even
* when You're able, You love us too much to always say yes.

Psalm 19:10–14, 119:29–40

Show me the right noes for this kid for this moment—whether dollar-aisle goodies, sugar or caffeine rushes, social media—so we can get to the right yeses. Help me prize the long game of what's best rather than this kid's bottomless appetites.

Still: My overcontrol cripples their hearts from developing from the inside out. Pry off my hot little hands when I'm controlling outcomes or consequences I shouldn't. Don't let me spare my kids rich life lessons of resilience. Problem-solving. Competence and confidence learned only from overcoming. My own trust in them.

You know my worst, bubble-wrapped parenting emerges from that grippy hand of fear—rather than wisdom, patience, faith in You, and thoughtfully loving my kids. Keep me from mistaking overprotectiveness for healthy nurture and management. (Not to mention that if I hold this horse too tightly, it'll buck.)

My kids will eventually need to press through and into pain with trust, rather than avoiding or denying it. Let me value and pursue the gifts and character acquired in darkness. Teach me to raise strong kids who fully grieve, yet get up again after loss, now and in the future.

Romans 5:3–5; James 1:2–3, 12; 2 Corinthians 4:17

It's possible my kids, losing something they desperately want, may gain something they'll desperately need.

You know when and why I'm tempted to be a bona fide control freak. Maybe it's from perfectionism and performance: that failure's not an option. Keep me from scolding, excessive force, sky-high expectations, and dumb rules. I want a mask-free home where we all come as we are, not as we (or as I?) wish we were: like You welcome me. Guide my kids to that spacious place to grow and change, of blooming toward You, that is grace.

Romans 5:8, 15:7

Even when I'm scared spitless.

amen.

Unpack *My* **Anxiety** *from Their* **Sleepover Bag**

To the One Who Never Sleeps,

Why does parenthood feel like "forever to have your heart go walking around outside your body"?[5]

This child is blessedly oblivious, innocent, popping up and down like a Super Ball. And here I am, restraining myself from chewing my cuticles until they bleed, fake-smiling in a way I hope doesn't resemble the Joker.

Out loud, I'm asking if this kid remembered their toothbrush and medication. Inside, my brain is flying around a hamster wheel.

I don't want my child to be hurt in ways that could take years to heal. By unsafe or unkind people, including but not limited to kids making dumb decisions.

But I'm grateful, too: for my child's friends and the priceless gift of belonging. Of being chosen by their peers for the chance to connect and experience hospitality.

As much as I'm sure my child would love to have me tag along like an extra appendage to every possible life circumstance through adulthood—maybe it's not such a good idea? I'm guessing my kid could use some karaoke and laser tag without me. But knowing when to remove the training wheels, literal and metaphorical, is an exercise in wisdom. Please hand me Your discernment about appropriate and inappropriate risks.

Let Your Holy Spirit be present in and protective of my child when some kid suggests they have "an awesome idea" involving a really stupid one.

Romans 12:21

Help my child not to be overcome by evil but to overcome evil with good—including being kind when others are boneheads. Glad You're the God who never sleeps, who keeps us from all harm and watches over our lives day and night.

Psalm 121:4, 6–7

Maybe my fears are kicking up old areas of pain. Pull me to a new level of being able to turn to You with deep-seated cares. I commit them to You afresh when this person, more precious than my own life, walks out onto what I see as a battlefield. You've cared for me when I was vulnerable and underequipped. You've been our dwelling place in all generations.

Psalm 90:1

So please protect this kid from irrational fear. Including mine.

I pray for Your protection—from other people and my own child, from themselves—and that this kid would have a crazy-good time involving minimal shaving cream and no freezing of underwear. Allow me to be gracious yet hold the line of respect and personal responsibility when they come home grumpy from going to sleep at 3:42 a.m.

Amen.

Make Me Your Lamb, *Not a Mama Bear*

Fortress,

You saw what really happened. So would You be willing to help me advocate for my child without turning into a you-know-what?

I want my child to know someone fought for them when they were hurt; to glimpse You as Shield and Defender through me. I don't want to choose passivity or denial for lack of courage.

But You've shown me that sometimes my Justice Meter is just plain *off*. I want to advocate for what's right, what's true—not just blindly for my child.

Would You share Your wisdom and perspective with me? Pry defensiveness from my clutches. I want my child to take 100 percent responsibility for their contribution here, even if it's only 1 percent of the problem. Expose me to the whole story. And help me love Your long game for my child, the character produced by what's hard.

Protect me from decisions that I may later regret. Keep top of mind how my response could affect how my child's treated in the long run.

But even more, I'm playing out for this kid how to handle conflict on an adult level. You reconciled my relationship with You through Jesus. And You give me the mission of reconciliation—to show people Your heart.

2 Corinthians 5:18–20

So I'm advocating not just for my child but for You.

Show me how to turn this into "all of us against the problem," not us against each other. Steer me clear of us/them categories that dehumanize and judge the other person, categories keeping me from empathy and humility. Let the Golden Rule filter my mouth. The false justice of gossip and smear campaigns has no place here; vengeance belongs to You. Not me. You've got big feelings about forgiveness. Guess that means I should delete the nasty text I've been mentally composing?

Romans 12:17–19

Matthew 18:21–35

Not gonna lie—my mouth could really get me in trouble right now. Duct-tape me from saying what doesn't build up or extend Your undeserved kindness; from what's not appropriate for this situation. I may require fairly severe help to issue a peace-loving, gentle answer.

Ephesians 4:29

Proverbs 15:1

Bottom line, help me protect like You do—and overcome evil with good. Get me out of this person's face, and keep me looking at Yours.

Romans 12:21

Amen.

The 1 a.m. *(and Maybe 4 a.m. Again)* Prayer

Father,

Psalm 121:4

I am so glad I don't need to nudge You and ask, "Hey, are You awake?" You never doze off as You watch over Your kids.

But I know You don't want me pulling all-nighters. (You've seen me tired and grumpy—definitely not my holiest self.) I do appreciate the whole rest-rhythm You've set up for my body and soul.

Yet somehow in the darkness, fear for my own kids sneaks in and sits on my chest. I can't stop my mind cycling through all the kid what-ifs and parenting to-dos—none of them ending in rainbows. The stakes for my children feel sky-high. And man, could I use the sleep before I try to jump those hurdles.

Isaiah 26:3

Psalm 23

Deep down, I realize that if and when I put my trust in You, You wrap me in perfect peace. You offer me Your protection and direction. And You walk with me through every dark place—real and imagined. You never let go, never let me down.

But as I flip my pillow and wrestle with the covers, I often forget and parent as if my hustle (rather than Your grace) is what keeps our family going.

If I know how to worry, I know how to meditate, right?[6] Help me snag each anxious thought zipping through my mind right now and toss it over to You—because You love my kids and me so stinkin' much. You're always ready to scoop us up in Your arms and point us toward the night-light out of the darkness. You even have the (Living) water we actually need!

2 Corinthians 10:5, 1 Peter 5:7, Psalm 55:22

John 1:5, Ephesians 6:12

Guide me to breathe in Your peace and breathe out my anxiety . . . about which I can do very little. Settle my restless soul in the way only You can—no matter how calming my weighted blanket and cooling sheets can feel.

Luke 11:25

Soothe my fears with reminders of Your love and hand in every situation. Tuck me in with Your strength so that I trust You and surrender my grip on (and worries about!) the big and little moments. I want to let You be God, by day and by night. I believe in Your mercies for the new day . . . and pray they include good, strong coffee.

Psalm 77:12

Lamentations 3:23

amen.

Teach Me to Launch *(and Not Lose It in the Process)*

God with Us,

Whether they're climbing on a school bus for the first time or piling into an old beater with friends who can shave and drive, watching this kid grow up is killing me softly. Outside I'm smiling and waving; inside I'm throwing myself in front of the bumper.

Truthfully, from the minute the doc cut the cord, they were increasingly outside of reach. My control trickles like an hourglass, even though I love them as if they were still attached to my body. In their series of baby, elementary, then middle-schooler steps, I did know this goal from the beginning: launching them into the world as people who love You with their lives. Like You launch Your kids.

Matthew 10:16–17

But the radius is increasing: I'm releasing them more and more into Your care. And it feels like running buck naked through a hailstorm. Not that I have done this specifically. Though I imagine it resembles sending this child off to prom, or maybe to ride bikes unchaperoned in the park.

You don't promise smooth sailing but the opposite. Yet You've overcome this world. And You offer me Your peace. So please, let me lean hard into that unexplainable soul-tranquility.

John 16:33

2 Corinthians 10:5, Philippians 4:6–7, Ephesians 3:17–19

When anxiety is grating my liver, let me throw every request before the One who loves this kid and loves me more than I can grasp. Set up a night watch around my heart, capturing every rogue thought. Including but not limited to *What if some kid tries to sell them drugs and their only way to say no is to be eaten by a bear?* And *Not texting back = dead.*

Galatians 5:25

Instead, let me champion independence and cheer this child on in becoming a person distinct from me, yet more like You. Move me to keep in step with Your Holy Spirit and His pace in this child's life.

Dial back any of my inappropriate control when this kid "can't wait for that sleepover!" or hopes to flip burgers after school. Especially control which could shut down our collaboration, along with their sense of competence, trustworthiness, and confidence in someday becoming an adult. (There are worse things than failure, imperfection, and even pain.) Grant me vision of both this child and Your care for them, big enough to overwhelm my fear and, yes, loss.

In all grief or mild terror, drive me closer to Your heart—and to appreciation of the beautiful moments that are still ours to hold: past, present, future. Even if, occasionally, they're concealed by reeking piles of laundry.

amen.

Jesus, Take *the* Wheel

Refuge, Stronghold, Fortress, Deliverer . . .

I'm teaching my child to drive, so let's just say I'm gripping Your names tighter than my seat belt right now. Plan on me calling on You a lot throughout this journey.

I'm sure, within my white-knuckled grasp of the "Lord Help Us" panic handle, there are gems to be mined about parenting and control. But mostly I'm just reflexively pressing my foot into the floorboard as if an imaginary brake will save us all.

It's only a matter of time before my child holds a shiny, terrifying license. Meanwhile, I must counterintuitively expose them to as many real-life situations as I can (Rain! Merging! Ice! Stop-and-go traffic! Pedestrians in slo-mo!). Soon they will commandeer the wheel, solo, of heavy machinery traveling at sixty-five miles per hour, perhaps complete with Spotify blasting "Fast Car," dripping burrito in hand.

At some point, I have to hand over the keys and vacate the passenger seat, unless I want to chauffeur this child's minivan when they're forty. In general, it is good they learn. At least that's what I'm telling myself.

But the risks, for my child and that oncoming car, are legit.

One go-to thought: From before I knew this child existed, a thousand things had to go right. Surely that number is in the trillions by now, with every inhale and exhale, every heartbeat, every cell that divided. And You have driven them all. No rogue molecule exists in Your universe.[7] This child has always belonged far more to You than myself or themselves.

I also know You permit the consequences of our actions. So I ask first for wisdom for myself and my child—including the character and discernment for even split-second decisions. Help my child truly understand the power of this set of keys for short- and long-term good and harm. Don't let them overestimate their ability. Protect my child from the influence of the unwise and destructive. Instead, let this vehicle be a holy place of kindness and connection with You.

James 1:5

Romans 12:3

Proverbs 1:10, 4:14–15, 13:20; 1 Corinthians 10:30

And I'm not just talking my stream-of-consciousness prayers as my child hops the curb. Again.

Meanwhile, expose my child to the know-how they'll need. Maintain my own heart in a place of peace, patience, and slowness to anger, like You maintain toward me. You are my safety net. In mercy, preserve the lives and health of all who come in or near our vehicle(s).

Exodus 34:6, Romans 2:4, 1, Timothy 1:16

Psalm 25:15

Help me trust You, and help me convey that trust to my child. Especially the next time they attempt to turn left.

amen.

Protect Their Hearts *and* My Blood Pressure

My Shield,

I've seen—I've *had*—that starry-eyed, lovesick look before. And man, the hormones flying around here make a parent want to duck and cover. I may or may not be considering a titanium chastity belt for this kid. It'll be trendsetting. Trust me.

Truth: Romantic relationships take so very much emotional maturity in exceedingly delicate areas with high stakes. Communication skills. Conflict. Character judgment. Melodrama management!

What's Your heart for my child here?

I ask for wisdom on managing the progression of my child's gradual maturity (or lack thereof?) from texting to group dates to young-adult trust levels. Help us form intelligent boundaries together around shared values: barriers to their being hurt, manipulated, used, disturbed.[8]

★Proverbs 4:23

Galatians 5:22, Philippians 2:3–4, Hebrews 5:14, James 1:5

Psalm 34:3

Please guard this kid's heart and body, even when they're hawking them at bargain-basement prices. I ask You to give them generous wisdom, discernment, self-control, the skills to love their neighbor as themselves. Let them honor You together with people they date.

1 Samuel 16:7

You see beyond appearances, to the heart . Generate attraction to people of thriving faith who love You with their lives.

You know what my kid craves—whether affirmation, identity, gratification, affection, commitment, respect . . . arm candy, glowy validation during the zits-and-braces years. Every other standard I'd love to set (like, no dating until you're thirty-seven and no riding in cars with back seats) falls prey to the sucking holes in my kids' hearts. Holes only You can fill.

So satisfy them at a heart level—to the point they no longer claw for those things through romantic relationships. Jeremiah 2:13, Psalm 90:14

You protect the simple. So, would You please (oh please) run interference on dumb decisions, especially those with sweeping consequences? Psalm 116:6 Keep this pheromone-laden pre-adult in step with Your Holy Spirit. Galatians 5:25

If and when this kid messes up, let me communicate the redemption, healing, and wholeness Jesus made possible.

This kid's not under this roof much longer. Make me a conversation-starter rather than a conversation-stopper. Give us opportunities to humbly sort through what's valuable about their experiences, triumphs, screwups, what they want in a mate, what to steer clear of.

Guess I need to scrap the plans for the 24/7 body cam?

Amen.

Prevent Me *from* Searching *the* Ditches

Protector,

So curfew was then, and this is now. And even a "BTW, I'm not dead" text would go a long way at this moment.

I'm army-crawling through an emotional mash-up of fear and fury. Trying to think of the last time I looked forward this much to an eye-rolling teenager turning the doorknob.

Seeing as You are the Prince of Peace, I ask for Your ability to take every thought captive and help me surrender it to You. In other words, please harness the stampede of statistically unlikely yet decidedly vivid worst-case scenarios galloping through my brain.

2 Corinthians 10:5a

(Provided this kid is not dead on the side of the road, You may need to protect them from me. Hell hath no fury like a freaked-out parent.)

Truth is, there may be an entirely rational reason why this kid is . . . wherever You can see them . . . and not ninja-creeping through the back door. Help me to listen *before* I go nuclear on this child.

Remind me what it feels like to be a teenager, and maybe to lack a fully developed frontal lobe. Remind me where I put mine so I can walk in Your Holy Spirit rather than opting for vigilante justice with this kid.

When they walk in the door, fill me first with gratitude. But for the time being, remind me of Your sweeping, utter faithfulness—and that You're far better able to protect and deliver this child than I am. You need not have location services enabled to see them, speak into their ear, and even take the wheel (literally or metaphorically).

Keep this child and those around them safe and making wise decisions, including but certainly not limited to: neither adding to nor subtracting from the population, going the speed limit, and saying no to stupidity in every form.

Vengeance is Yours . . . but, y'know, I could have Your back. Just say the word.

Amen.

Guide Us *to Thy* **Perfect Sitter**

Everlasting Father,

This is a good thing—that my life incorporates activities outside of parenthood. (Truth: Part of me can't wait.) But I've read too many *Calvin and Hobbes* to believe all sitters are created equal in tolerance, trustworthiness, and lack of temptation to scroll their smartphones.

♡ *Jeremiah 17:10*

You see to the heart of every person. So with Your knowledge, please help me avoid the duds and delinquents. Especially those overcharging for it.

Would You guide me to a babysitter who's responsible, creative, and faithful? I need other voices in my kids' lives who model character, community, patience, kindness, and love for You.

People my kids and I can both trust and enjoy. People who play hide-and-seek, people who blow bubbles, people who both initiate craft projects and clean them up, people who are kind even when my kids act like hellions.

Psalm 139:7–12

When I can't be there, I know You are—and better than any nanny cam. Please keep my kids safe, my babysitter fully present, my mind at peace, and my budget intact.

Amen.

Prayers *for* Connection & Understanding

Send Down *the* Decoder Ring *to* This Kid

Creator,

Not gonna lie—this kid's different from the picture in my head. Different from me in general: sometimes as opposite as those old photo negatives.

Psalm 18:30, Isaiah 55:8–9

But Your ways are higher, perfect. You intricately, spectacularly planned this child, their ways, and their days even before their first gasp of breath.

Psalm 139:4, 14–16

I acknowledge right here and now that You may not share my vision or timing or pictured journey for this kid. Protect my child and me from the tragedy of me shoehorning this child into my image rather than Yours. Help me trust that every personality trait that drives me batty is exactly what You require to accomplish Your plans for this planet, our family, and Your own honor. Don't let me touch those.

My hope doesn't lie in my will accomplished in the form of a child. That will, that expectation, could easily become what I look to for worth, satisfaction, significance, fulfillment—instead of You. Only You, not my child, carry the substance to fill these holes within me.

Please, grant me wisdom and practical ways to connect with my child's world—their interests, personality, gifting, story, perspectives, and passion. Help me muscle beyond the melodrama or disorganization or introversion or persistence or flightiness causing me to gnash my teeth. Would You help me discover and understand the "whys" behind who my child is?

Generate gratitude and appreciation for the way You made them—in Your image—and guide me to worship You there. You entered my world, even when it jarred the senses and brimmed with fallenness. You weren't content with distance. I imagine that means as my parent, You'd listen to me chatter about my interests. You'd buy tickets or lessons for me, and clap the loudest. So help me, too, to perform the hard, intentional work of pursuing this child's heart. Whether it leads me through the makeup aisle or the Pokémon aisle.

John 1:14

Proverbs 23:26

Cause us to laugh together and carve out time to enjoy each other. Let any differences and conflict form us into more deeply understanding, welcoming people—more like You. Let our relationship take priority over our disagreement. Let me love them for who they are rather than who I wish them to be. Stop me from ever even hinting that my child needs to change their core or be like me for us to be close.

* Romans 15:7

Don't let me miss the sheer joy and wonder of my child, Your idea.

Amen.

Lead Us *to* Friends Who *Don't* Pick *Their* Noses

To the One Closer Than a Brother,

You know I love this kid more than my own life. But every now and then, it's nice to talk to someone whose meat I don't need to cut. Someone who doesn't ask me to wipe them.

I'm saying we both can use friends our own age. And we might even be . . . lonely.

You get it. Even when it was just You and Adam—no sin on the planet—You said it wasn't good that Adam was alone. But even before that, You were satisfied in community with Yourself: just the Three in One, forever.

I'm hoping for people my kids can depend on. You've seen my blind spots. I need voices other than my own, investing in this kid in ways I can't. And every now and then, when my kid does that one thing (You know the thing), I think it might be good if someone else were weighing in on social skills.

Your last prayer before the Cross was that Your people would be one in the way You are. Kind of a tall order. So maybe this sounds juvenile—but I'm asking You for true, long-standing, trustworthy friendships for me, my child, our family.

Matthew 18:21–35

Even if I've been burned, or resist forgiving. Or when it just feels easier to clam up and isolate, away from girl drama or kids with potty mouths.

I'm asking for people who love relentlessly and practically, on days when we're conquering the world, or when the world is definitely winning. Or when one of us might give or pursue more than the other. Or eras with as many melty beads on the floor as fingerprints on the mirror.

Acts 2:42–46

Looking at the early Church, You cast this vision of us being together holding all things in common, devoting ourselves to each other and eating together. Restoring each other. My family may not be quite there yet . . . ? I may need Your help to be generous and fully present with people. Or to slide down the mask that sometimes feels more comfortable than my own face. Exchange my image management for connection.

Philippians 2:25–30

Is this the point where I should admit a social media status update doesn't fill my tank?

Whether it's picking up the phone or bringing over Popsicles, give my child and me courageous and creative ideas to take initiative. And to keep taking initiative when we're met with a chorus of crickets chirping. Together—even if we're introverts and lovin' it—show us how to build a family culture of including others and inviting community.

Maybe I should shower first?

amen.

Bless This New Sibling *(Though They're Not a Puppy)*

Giver of Life,

Thank You for creating this person in front of us and knowing they are just what our family needs—even though at least one of us was hoping for a puppy. You wrote every one of this kid's days before they even showed up. Thank You for all the little miracles it took to make life and to bring this child to us as part of Your perfect plan.

Psalm 139:16

Make our arms strong for the tasks ahead. Kids and their bodies take a Lot. Of. Work. You haul each of us into this world needing community and connection just to survive. Let us show each other what Your all-in love looks like and truly embrace this wacky new normal. (Even if a new pet sounded like more fun to some.)

Proverbs 31:17, 2 Peter 1:3

Loving someone well is a pretty great way to be overwhelmed. But through knowing You, we are given everything for the task You're asking of us.

Fill us with stamina and intentionality for the hard work in front of us, of loving this human. When we want to grumble, swap it for gratitude. When we feel snippy, hand us long-suffering. When we're freaking out, whisper Your pervasive peace over and over, reminding us You're trustworthy. When we're tempted to be lazy, let us lean in like You. Especially when someday this child spectacularly ticks us off and/or embarrasses us—doing that one thing You already know they're going to do. (Go big or go home, right?)

As Hannah dedicated Samuel to You, we offer this child's life to be all Yours, as a holy and precious gift. Don't let a day go by without surrounding this child (and our family) with Your presence.

1 Samuel 1:22, 27–28

Would You show us all how to know and rely on Your love? Especially when we mess up? (It's coming.)

1 John 4:16

Bring this child to know and love You completely from a young age; shape their soul, and let it be soft and responsive to You. You are this child's true parent. Raise them to be brave, wise, loving, generous, and a demonstration of Your undeserved kindness toward humans. Even when humans are so much less than nice.

Romans 5:8

Spoiler alert: You put this child in a very imperfect, weird family. Throughout life, surround this child with people who compensate for the ways we're not like You, and with people who will draw out Your image in this child. You've already authored good works for this child to do, according to Your workmanship; let them do no more, no less.

Ephesians 4:29

Surely I wasn't this much work, right?

amen.

Deliver Us *from* Our Devices

Ever-Present One,

Too often it feels like screen time is controlling my family rather than the other way around. And when it's taken away? You'd think I cut off the kid's pinkie toe. Agony! Thrashing! Tears!

I'm not for banning all gratuitous fun. I know that through my structure and healthy boundaries, my kids need to learn self-discipline with tech, to survive in their future. So empower me to teach them what healthy amounts of fun stuff look like—as a privilege to be regulated or even earned through trustworthiness, accountability, responsibility.

You give us a Spirit of power, love for each other, and self-control. But Lord, have mercy. What a beast. Show me how to skillfully keep tech in its proper place. Remind me to continually ask: Will this tech help us become less foolish, more wise? Less fearful, more courageous?[9]

2 Timothy 1:7

I want to take this role of discipling, forming, and nourishing my kids seriously—rather than handing that role to a streaming service. I want full, satisfying lives for our days. But is this the right time to confess this bewitching digital babysitter hands me space to take a breath or schedule the next dental cleaning? These days are *loooong*. Remind me the years are short.

Help our home grow comfortable with quiet. I mean, the pace of some of these programs and apps feels like one step away from seizure-inducing. If my kids' brains are trained like this, how will they learn to listen to Your still, small voice?

To help them feel their way toward You, I want to train their ears to listen, their eyes to see deeper. Show me how to cultivate kids who pay attention to Your presence and what You're powerfully enacting around them (to Your credit, better than any video game). Help me raise kids capable of deep rather than superficial, tech-like relationships and thought.[10] Let us be present in the here and now, thoughtfully spending this one life to live,[11] with embodied people face-to-face.[12] And not with a screen, not feeling "off" without constant stimulation.

Acts 17:27

But . . . maybe I'm modeling that steady scroll of distraction. You ask me to be watchful, alert, and self-disciplined. And we become like what we behold. What do we love to watch—and therefore worship?[13] Show me how to limit my own devices, and what desires fuel my habits—whether entertainment and novelty, fear, ego, the desire to be liked, FOMO. Or maybe I'm avoiding boredom. Responsibility. Hardship.[14]

1 Corinthians 16:13–14

Let us see You for the captivating Creator You are. Forget the 3D or 4K effects. You're the Three in One.

amen.

Harmonize *the* Homework Hour

Great Peacemaker,

School has, perhaps, received the blossom of my kids' days, and here I am, making the most of the stem. They forage for processed food and take out the day's tension on the family member (or pet) in closest proximity.

In short, we are cranky.

Mark 12:30–31, Psalm 133:1–3

But You desire more than for us to just army-crawl to dinner. We'd both like to see at least a little love shared. It's pretty great when families live in genuine unity.

In place of the backpacks that just crashed on my floor, let these kids put on compassion, kindness, humility, and patience. Extend us all the ability to put up with and forgive each other like You've forgiven us, banishing snark and sass. Over all of this, help us put on love. We want Your peace ruling the day even more than touchiness, taunting, and tiredness.

Colossians 3:12–15

Father, what do my kids need right now?

They're more than what they produce or accomplish, more than machines. Before they're back to the grindstone of homework, how could I help restore them, like You restore us?

Psalm 23:3

Maybe those "green pastures" mean some running around in the yard. Maybe "still waters" look like my child doing nothing productive for a hot minute. It's possible comfort looks like a hug, or plopping on the sofa to hear about the day over sips of chocolate milk, or shaking my head at a way they felt bruised today. Rather than driving my kids, let me lead them like You do. Perhaps I prepare a table of crackers and cheese for them in the presence of their worst day. Psalm 23:1–5

Even within the chaos, You run after us with goodness and unswerving love. We'd love to give it back to You in the way we treat each other and pull close to You.

So set the tone for this three-ring circus. It's all Yours. Even in the midst of broken pencil lead and flying fruit snacks.

Welcome to the jungle.

amen.

For *When* My Spouse Is *(Of Course)* So Wrong

God of Reconciliation,

Is it appropriate for me to ask for You to lift the veil of blindness for this person *so clearly* in the wrong? Yeah, didn't think so.

Still, I'm coming to You with all the ugly emotions. Frustration. Disappointment. Fear. Guilt. Exhaustion. Feeling unseen, underappreciated, unacknowledged. Annoyance at my spouse's lack of empathy or logic. Sometimes my spouse's arguments feel like reading the double-digit pages of the "Terms of Use." Eventually, I just give up and click "I Agree."

John 14:6, 1 John 3:20

But You know better than I do my motives and true concerns. Even those I can't admit to myself. You're the One who actually sees truth. And that truth is likely much larger and more complex than what I can see (don't tell my spouse just yet).

Proverbs 3:5–6

I want to acknowledge You and Your ways. Even more than I want to be right. Which is a lot. So can You please make our parenting paths straight and guide us to not lean on our own understanding?

Romans 5:8, 2 Corinthians 5:18–21

Truth is, our conflict is a chance to understand each other and grow. To honor You with how we treat each other. To show the world—and each other—how You responded when we were Your enemies. Which, thankfully, may not have involved throwing hands up in the air and informing someone exactly how dumb their parenting ideas are.

Would You (a) soften my heart, moving me away from pride and into deep humility? And (b) give me wisdom to know what I'm getting wrong and not seeing here?

I confess my disproportionate desire for the last word. Particularly to hear, "I'm sorry. You're right."

But You see what hovers beneath my spouse's emotion or arguments, too: experiences, history, conflicting desires, key values we're each protecting. In Your wisdom, You made us both parents of this kid. Two are better than one. We need each other.

Ecclesiastes 4:9–10

1 Corinthians 12:21

So I ask You for a heart in both of us that listens, sees, and receives both You and each other. Give us not just fake peace but unity of mind. Show us where to go when we reach an impasse. And no matter what, help us put on compassionate hearts, kindness, humility, meekness, and patience.

1 Peter 3:8

Colossians 3:12

Basically, keep me from saying that astonishingly witty and biting zinger (yep, that one).

Amen.

Reveal *the* Feels Beneath *"I'm Fine"*

Engineer of Emotion,

If this kid were a duck, they'd be floating peacefully on the surface right now—and paddling furiously beneath. Whether I know the cause or not, I'm getting the vibe of serious emotion churning somewhere within. Not sure why it hasn't made it out yet, but pulling us toward truth and a relationship with You seems to be one of Your infinite fortes.

I see You experiencing the whole spectrum of emotion, both in Your Word and during Your time in our skin. Feelings are a vivid part of Your image. Even when we don't use them in ways that reflect You. (Emotions aren't the problem; our flesh is.)[15]

Would You give me ideas to help this kid feel and deal rather than stuff and bluff? (When one's crush dumps them during passing period, the dumpee is not "fine.")

Psalm 51:6

We welcome You into our deepest, most uncomfortable, or confusing parts—not in spite of them. Emotions don't get left outside You. Telling the truth, including about where we're at, is crucial to relationship with You.

Deuteronomy 6:4; Psalm 56:8; Matthew 5:8, 15:7–9, 22:37–39

Close the gap between our hearts and appearances. Pull down our masks when we need Your comfort. Because we know You collect our tears in Your bottle.

Yet because we also want to love others well through our emotions, let us withhold displays of emotion (looking at you, hulking green monster of rage) when it honors You and the occasion.

We all need help managing feelings rather than them managing us. Help us get and stay real about our driving motivations and emotions, channeling them through Your Word instead. (As the saying goes, emotions are like kids: Don't let them drive the car, but don't stuff them in the trunk, either.)[16]

Your presence is where our nervous systems and feelings can recover a healthy equilibrium, and eventually even joy and peace. That's our superpower. You receive us and restore us—whether we bomb the test after six hours of studying, fall on the ice right smack-dab in front of a full school bus, or airball what would have been the winning goal.

Psalm 16:11, 23:1–3; Nehemiah 8:10

Walking on the road to Emmaus with Your followers, You showed up as they told their stories, wading through shocking grief and broken hope. Be with my child like this—and help me do the same with my expressions, tone, willingness to listen, willingness to walk alongside.

Luke 24:13–32

Still: Lead us not into melodrama, but deliver us with bear hugs, a good night's sleep, and dark chocolate.

Amen.

When *in the* **Wilderness** *of* ***Minecraft*** **Levels** *and* **Private Parts**

Wonderful Counselor,

When it comes to What I Believe About Embarrassing, Hairy, or Mundane Topics with Children, theories are easier than wiping the freak-out off my face or blinking the glaze from my eyes. But I want to be the go-to person for the embarrassing, the tricky, the weird, the downright boring aspects of my child's world.

Deuteronomy 6:1–9

In truth, most of the mortifying questions will only get funkier as my child grows older. And You've tasked me with discipling my child: helping them meticulously, holistically form a biblical worldview. Practicality tells me this is assembled not once but piece by piece as we apply each issue to real life, Your Word informing us (rather than relaying this responsibility to a search engine or the locker room).

Do I really want my child pawing through their kid-sized toolbox—their best guess, their best friends, their best attempt to wing it?

Evil isn't just "out there." It's within my kids and me, because sin is part of us. So protecting my kids isn't enough. As Robin to Your Holy Spirit's Batman, I've gotta cultivate their consciences.

So. Inhale. Maintain eye contact.

Grant me the courage to view my child's questions as an open door to talk about Scripture as we "walk by the way," to the maximum level of what's age appropriate. Prevent me from glancing around for a fire escape. Instead, help me take my child's hand to navigate complexity, secure trust and honesty, and communicate that *I will always tell you the truth. I will always listen to you, no matter the required level of effort. Your questions and thoughts are worthy of my interest and response. Come to me with anything. I will show up.* Deuteronomy 6:7

My kids need vocabulary to talk maturely about emotions, sticky situations, money, sex, and real life. They require wisdom and discernment if they're going to stand strong amidst peers or lies—and if they're going to fully comprehend how Scripture teaches, corrects, trains, and equips. My child needs to know that what concerns them is worth my time. 2 Timothy 3:16–17

Mirroring Yours—grant me presence, patience, and wisdom in the long-winded, the less-than-appropriate, and, for heaven's sake, the puberty and sex questions. Please rally my unshocked or highly interested face, as appropriate, when I can't remember where I put it.

Amen.

Gather Us Together
with Leftovers and Love

Daily Bread,

As we lay down our foam dart guns, overstuffed backpacks or inboxes, and drama of group chats and the day, collecting our family around this table, we find ourselves alone with each other and You.

Thank You for a decent, uncharred meal that brings us together. It's just a crumb of Your own prepared place for us, and the wedding feast where we someday long to raise a glass. Meanwhile, You provide comfort, peace, laughter, nurture that we can taste, smell, touch. Even when our cuisine is a bit subpar.

*Matthew 10:42

Let us do the same, offering a cold cup of water in Your name.

Lamentations 3:22–23, Matthew 6:11, John 6:35

We're grateful for food and time together that nourish and satisfy these ever-hungry bodies and souls. They're a glimpse of the true and better Bread You are, the kitchen open to us around the clock, fresh daily.

Psalm 139:16, 145:15–16; Matthew 6:31–32; Luke 12:24–26

And thanks, too, for the crazy crew clustered around these plates. We admit that we may not have seen eye to eye every moment of today. But Your wisdom put us together, asking us to do the hard work of loving and leaning toward each other.

More than activities dictating our schedules, teach us to choose time and presence. Show us how to truly, deeply connect with and understand each other, even when we have no idea where to start.

This includes but is not limited to being grouchy, touchy, or annoying; failing to faithfully bathe or brush teeth; scattering personal belongings throughout the house like confetti at a parade; hogging the remote; and saying dumb things. You give us a steady diet of patience, forgiveness, and mercy; help us do the same, even when it's straight-up painful, hard, or inconvenient.

As we chow, let us show and tell the stories of what You've done and who You are. We open the door to You here. Come eat with us. Even when we argue like it's going out of style.

Revelation 3:20

amen.

To *the* Patron Saint *of* Sturdy Doors

Opener When We Knock,

I've been shut out. Real or metaphorical, there's a closed door between this child and me.

Part of me may want to wheedle or cajole. Or sweat and chew my nails. Or bait them with pizza. Or force my way in, figurative guns blazing. Gotta say, I'm not a fan of stonewalling (at least on this side of the equation).

Deuteronomy 6:4, John 17:21

Here's what I know: You love unity. You *are* unity—the Three in One. You hold all things together—including this scattered mind and this scattered family. Mind lending a hand?

Colossians 1:17

You know this kid's story: why they're turned away, or hiding. You're present with me here, them there. Grant me insight into their emotions and responses, why they'd rather be alone than together, and what this is really about. Beneath my anger, hurt, or fear, generate curiosity as to why I'm staring at this obstinate plank of wood rather than my child's eyes.

Psalm 139:7–17

This barrier is the opposite of what I want with this child. I want to know and understand and receive. But it's my child's story to tell. Rather than manipulating or demanding, let me treat their emotions—including those beneath the anger—with the kindness and respect You show me. Even when my child is childish, malicious, suspicious, vicious.

Jeremiah 31:3; Romans 2:4, 9:18

I need Your ideas and rapport to regain trust and hold that trust as sacred—yet refrain from multitasking as a doormat.

In Your hand, You hold all hearts involved. Make them soft all the way around. Mine. This child's. Any other involved parties. Show me any contribution of mine, and how to repent . . . without groveling. * Proverbs 16:9, 21:1

Whether this kid needs a cool-off or there's a bridge to be built, loan me patience for the long game. I don't just want my child to spill the tea or contribute to breezy family interactions. I long to earn an invitation to a more intimate relationship by mirroring Your trustworthiness.

Help us reach toward each other, even when one of us is more comfortable there inside Fort Knox. You're the best at this. In fact, You become the Door for us; You open doors no one can shut. You know what it's like to go the distance to bring Your kids close. John 10:7 Revelation 3:8

Even when it feels like trying to reach through a wall.

Amen.

Help Us Like Each Other *Before We Get to* Church

Lord of the Sabbath,

I could say that I have a bone to pick with the inventor of Sunday mornings, but we both know Who that is. So I respectfully decline. You and I both know the problem lies further down the food chain. Between spilled cereal bowls, locating the other shoe of the only pair my child will agree to wear, and that one kid falling in the diaper pail: We do need You today, Jesus.

Matthew 5:23

But I know (a) You ask us to patch things up with each other before worship, and (b) our dented, glowering little hearts might need a reset before singing anything praiseworthy.

So show me how to help my kids sift through the lives You've given, especially in the last week, for gratitude. Tip our eyes up from our own belly buttons—because You're worthy of worship. You've earned it, hands down. Let the chaos of this day, family, and season turn us toward You and Your words rather than away.

Mark 4:19

Tug us into forgiveness of each other. And even when we're wrestling with negative emotions (I'm looking at you, teenage angst), we ask that like David, Jesus, and Elijah, we bring our questions and feelings into Your sanctuary.

I am particularly glad that You love us and want us as we are, not as we wish we were. You want to engage with us even in the dark areas. Or just the grumpy, oversensitive, hormone-fueled, chocolate-stained, eye-rolling ones.

Isaiah 53:6; Romans 5:6, 8; 8:38–39

Settle Your peace and Your unity on this imperfect, beloved crew. You deserve our worship and attention much more than the device I just confiscated.

Amen.

Send People *My Child Listens to* Better Than Me

Community Creator,

Turns out I am far from perfect or even perfectly well-rounded. (Let's not broadcast it just yet.) My fabulous strengths have flip-side flaws I shouldn't copy-and-paste into another generation. Parenting is distinctly not a personal project but a community one.[17]

Plus, every now and then sparks fly (not the good kind). Perhaps my voice resembles wah-wah-wah, and someone else's hipness, turns of phrase, experiences, or other genius would resonate more than the person driving homework, chores, character, sibling reconciliation, the family car. Plus deafening relational static.

1 Corinthians 12:21

Though made in Your image, I'm a single part of Your Body. Maybe the spleen? To represent You fully and really raise this kid to look like You, I need Your Body. Your whole family. And not just because casseroles are nice.

Mark 6:3, Ephesians 2:19–22, 1 John 3:1–2

Via coaches, mentors, teachers, group leaders, other parents, neighbors, relatives, or tattooed/man-bunned/pierced and otherwise much cooler people from church, shape my kids to be more like Jesus, and invest in them. Open my possessive, threatened fingers.

Amen.

Prayers *for* Wisdom & Guidance

Lord, *Are You Sure* **I'm Qualified?**

Perfect Parent,

This may be a good time to confess that I am winging it as a parental figure. (Don't tell the kids.)

Sometimes my child brings home a really tough question, and I wonder how I have suddenly become this person who pays taxes, wishes they could go to bed earlier, wears boring shoes, and, every now and then, reminds me of one of my parents. Not in the good way.

Should I really be considered the expert in this situation? I was in junior high, like, yesterday.

But here's what I know: In Your wisdom, You appointed me as this kid's parent. I am a little shocked You made this decision on purpose.

2 Peter 1:3–4

I try to reassure myself that You give us everything we need for the life You want for us simply by our knowing You. One prayer that always seems to get a yes from You is a genuine plea for Your generous wisdom. I just need to believe You'll actually give it. And that it extends to the most treacherous territories—like kids' questions about sex, politics, and what happens to pets when they die.

James 1:5–6

Psalm 121:3

Keep my steps from slipping—at least metaphorically. Guard my mouth against bad advice popping out like a gumball from a prize machine. And let me feel Your Holy Spirit anointing me (me!) for the parenting tasks that feel incredibly tough . . . maybe even heavy.

1 John 2:20, 27

Remind me that You wove me into Your family's fabric and You delight in my honest (though often clumsy) offerings. Invite me to come to You in prayer when I'm feeling inadequate. Because the doubts in my head are asking that instead of having invisible faith, I lean on the worldly reality I perceive. And that looks like a spectacular crash and burn ahead on my part.

Help me listen to You, who's chosen me for good works You prepared in advance for me. And give me power to shut down the voice that tells me I shouldn't be operating heavy machinery or managing hormonal teenage angst or receiving the trust of this kid's wide eyes.

Ephesians 2:10

In embracing my weakness—which You have also ordained—You say I am blessed. You say Your power is perfect, resting on me when I don't have any. Considering the frequent train wrecks of my parental efforts, I could say I am one incredibly blessed, powerful person right now.

Matthew 5:3

2 Corinthians 12:9–10

May I sense Your wisdom flowing through me and into my parenting dilemmas . . . as strongly as I sense my profound inadequacy in the face of burned lasagna, teaching kids about sex, explaining national politics, and convincing the kids to put the toilet seat down.

Amen.

Keep *Our Family from* **Becoming** *a* **Viral Video**

Wonderful Counselor,

Why do kids feel so primed to utterly mortify parents? Maybe kicking this thing off with someone peeing on a stick should've tipped us all off.

Then comes the four-alarm meltdown in the housewares aisle. Poking Grandma's arm dangle. Asking at full volume whether the person in front of us has boy parts or girl parts.

In fact, if I weren't embarrassed in some of those moments, maybe something would be amiss.

But sometimes I'm embarrassed just because this kid is so different from me: the melodrama, the extroversion, the introversion. Guess a parent can hope their child's proclivity for performing show tunes while cartwheeling would stay within the family and out of the store's freezer section just a little while longer.

Ugh, how does healthy parental management devolve into a sheer desire to control so easily? Am I conforming this kid to my image rather than Yours?

Really, I want my kids to love Your good ways more than they love my image management. When my identity hinges on their performance, that screams dysfunction. (But can I tell You the stress sweat is real right now?)

Help me pinpoint whether there's an issue of morality or rudeness or unloving behavior I need to curb. And how I should discipline differently for childish behavior versus outright rebellion.

You seem to have a lot of big thoughts on timing and seasons of life, including the setting and timing for what I say. So I could use Your wisdom not just on *what* to say but on *how* and *when* to say it. Please give me ideas on how to steer my child firmly out of this train wreck—especially if their brain needs a cooldown—appropriately exposing guilt without shaming them.

Proverbs 25:11, Ecclesiastes 3:1–8, Ephesians 4:29

Bring to mind the right questions to get to my child's heart once we're alone. I could use Your thoughts to help my child restore what was broken here, even if that's through a simple, heartfelt apology.

Reality is, this world needs something way more important than my perfect kids. They need kids and parents who know they need Jesus.

And parents who, cheeks aflame, can show their kids Your kindness that leads to repentance. Even when my child farts in an elevator.

Romans 2:4

Amen.

May I Resist *the Ultimate Parent* Cop-Out Line

Ruler of All,

I feel like *Because I said so* is always on my tongue. Such an easy phrase to flick out there, my authority no doubt generating vast wonder in the eyes of my children.

Ephesians 6:1–3

And to be fair, my kids need to recognize the authority You've laid on me. Their whole lives, they're going to sit beneath authority You've put in place. They need to obey me right away, all the way, because I'm ultimately teaching them to obey You. (Not to mention, behavior tacky in a three-year-old is way scarier in an out-of-control fifteen-year-old.)

Romans 13:1–2, 4

2 Corinthians 5:7

Certainly, there are times You call us to blind obedience; to walk by faith and not by sight. Yet even then, I trust You not just because You're great but because You are good. You long for us to be all-in on obedience because You *have our hearts*, and we know Your ways.

**Hebrews 3:9–10*

Show me how to gain my kids' trust like that—starting with loving, wise, thoughtful, holy character. By developmentally appropriate expectations. By granting dignity not to rebellion or manipulation but to my kids' legitimate questions and fears and desire to think for themselves.

Proverbs 23:36

Guess that means *Because I said so* doesn't go very far most of the time? (Sigh.)

That heart-level obedience—not just welding together little robots and managing their behavior—requires so much doggone *vigilance*. Consistency. Rapport. Involvement. Help me discern when it's right to leverage my authority, and when I'm just being . . . well, lazy. To be honest, I might be a better army general than a shepherd in some moments.

My kids' days are stuffed with opportunities for respectful submission to imperfect people carrying authority's weight: Difficult teachers. Traffic stops. Demanding employers. Irritating relatives. Extend my kids' wisdom for rare moments they shouldn't obey, when authority's command falls contrary to Yours.

Healthy submission opens so many doors for my kids and builds respectful relationships. Even when I would like them *to just put the clothes in the hamper*, for the love of Mike.

Still, don't let me raise people pleasers or those who excuse unjust leadership but instead kids who can raise an honorable plea. Guide them to ultimately serve You as the highest authority.

Romans 12:10, Ephesians 6:6, Colossians 3:22

I want to shape kids who don't argue without appropriate respect, or grumble. Let them shine as lights in their generation . . . not flip others the bird.

Philippians 2:14–15

amen.

For *the* Crossing *of the* Chicken Nugget Desert

Lord of the Harvest,

You've creatively, startlingly gifted us an abundant variety of food on planet Earth. And yet here we are, prying open the box of fish sticks (again). Or the can of pasta rings drowning in questionably authentic tomato-ish sauce.

Deliver me from the dreaded picky eaters. (Does my kid eating a food count if I must first drown it in ranch dressing?)

Psalm 131:2, Philippians 4:12, 1 Thessalonians 5:18, 1 Timothy 6:6

I straddle the tension of shaping a grateful, content, decidedly non-entitled child—and the reality that this kid could quite possibly out-starve the apocalypse. For the sake of future generations, I will triumph in my resistance to being a child's short-order chef! Yet scurvy is a consideration.

Proverbs 19:18; 29:15, 17

So show me how to steadfastly bridge the gap between parenting for the long game, with the character You've commissioned me to develop—and the part of me that has better things to do than argue about a food deemed too wobbly, stinky, or green.

Grant my child some ever-loving flexibility. And deliver them from a limited world centered only around dishes paired with ketchup.

Amen.

Prayer *for a* **Lost Lovie**

All-Seeing One,

I acknowledge You know exactly where my child's lovie is hiding and how it got there. You also know what this object means to my child: my child's full history and attachment . . . and what would happen if we couldn't find it.

1 Peter 5:7, Matthew 6:32–33

I'm grateful You care about so much of what we care about with such detail—yet with so much more wisdom and perspective.

Psalm 139:1–3

We trust You know every movement of our bodies. In Your compassion, would You guide us to find what was lost? You seem to be really, really good at that.

Luke 15

And if, in Your wisdom, Your answer is no? Help us trust You. If needed, help me convey that trust amidst unanswered prayer to this child, knowing You love us both more than we can comprehend. We choose You—as Someone other than a cosmic vending machine for our desires.

Ephesians 3:17–19

Amen.

A Time to Discipline, *and a Time to Let It Slide*

Father of Our Souls,

Discipline ranks right up with adulting tasks like spending a paycheck on a water heater. Or agreeing to lance a boil. "Can't wait to discipline my kid!" said no (good) parent ever.

Help me see what I'm facing as a little present pain toward future holiness. I'm laying life's railroad tracks, allowing this kid to go places they never dreamed, and ideally empowering a lot of good with just the right level of structure.

*Hebrews 12:11

Because *oy*. We both know what underdisciplined kids are in for throughout life. "Off-roading" train = train wreck. (To be fair, some of my parenting days seem to meet that criterion.) You discipline because You love—at heart, You're gentle and wanting to guide.

Matthew 11:29, Hebrews 12:6–8

You tailor-make Your discipline—with the goal of making "disciples." And You're far more about this kid's heart response than mere behavior management. Remind me my goal isn't punishment. It's teaching—about Your kingdom. Not mine. I want to discipline as an extension of love, rather than "Woe unto thee for messing with the wrong parent!" Anyway, grounding "till either you're thirty-four or Jesus comes back" generally misses the point.

Hebrews 12:10

Matthew 23, 2 Corinthians 7:10

So I'm turning to You, Author of this kid. What's the best way to shepherd toward better future choices?

What's the "why" under the misdeeds here? Like, why did they just lick the top of the Parmesan shaker at the pizza joint? Is it rebelliousness, or just acting like a kid?

I need Your wisdom on what discipline they best respond to, misbehavior patterns, motivations and heart cravings beneath. When I don't know, help me ask the right questions *(What did you really want? What had control of your heart? What could you have done instead?)*. Let me use that knowledge for careful, scalpel-like discipline, rather than to just be an extra-clever jerk.

Show me how to replay how You love us and encounter our own sin. (So maybe discipline reveals how I perceive You responding to me?) Let my correction mirror Yours and aim to restore all that's been broken. Because of You, we're not slaves to sin. Let me convey hope rather than hopelessness, even when delivering deserved consequences.[18]

Romans 6:17–18, 1 Peter 2:24

Empower me toward healing words with a gentle tone that turns away anger. Hold me back from name-calling, imitation, sarcasm, swearing, sweeping statements, disparagement.

Proverbs 15:1

Even when this kid just lied about brushing their teeth. (Like I can't tell the difference.)

amen.

Be My Mouth Guard *on the* Sidelines

Divine Coach,

It's kinda fun, watching this kid tug on the potentially overpriced uniform, the cleats or sneakers, the clunky jumble of equipment. So thank You for the coach and their time and investment in my child, civic facilities offered for fun and development, and the ref I'm asking You to keep me from yelling at.

Between the water bottles, sunscreen, snacks, cowbell, and blankets, we may forget where we packed our patience. Or perspective. Excitement and emotions are high. Would You keep my family from being obnoxious?

Settle me from saddling my child with inappropriate expectations or demands—including parental idols of achievement, glory, approval, ego, or even anxiety about the future. There's no good part of this we didn't get from You. And You hold this kid's days and prospects in Your hand. So don't let my fears and "must-haves" steal this part of their childhood, with its freewheeling joy, peace, life lessons, camaraderie, and sheer fun.

1 Corinthians 4:7

Psalm 31:15

We ask that You give the referees justice; the coaches discernment around patience, encouragement, and nonshaming admonishment at the right times; the players excellence, wise decisions, protection, and sportsmanship, somewhere in the middle of all the adrenaline, sweat, and awkward team dynamics.

If and when my child, a teammate, an opponent, or others fall on their literal or metaphorical faces, grant me compassion and a vision beyond these couple of hours of my life. You're far more patient with me over far more consequential underperformance.

Allow me to value the skills learned in failure, loss, hardship, and even apparent injustice. Instill a powerful resilience in my child. I guess "You are dead to me!" shouted at a coach or ref could be considered less than classy?

When the buzzer sounds, there's one priority that conquers the rest: honoring You. This family chooses to dedicate any glory to You. If we manage to win without loving people, we gain nothing.

Psalm 115:1, Revelation 4:10–11

*1 Corinthians 13:1–3

So corral our attitudes in every moment of victory, defeat, tension, and huddling. Grant us kindness in the face of trash-talking, flying elbows, and even intentional roughhousing. Place in us Your heart for encouragement, respect, and perseverance.

1 Peter 3:9

And while You're there—any recommendations on a robust laundry detergent? I'm open to ideas from the ultimate authority on washing white as snow.

Amen.

O God, *Our* Help *in the* Blame Games

Wise Teacher,

I'm seeking to instruct my child—in things that may actually bode well for survival, future job retention, prevention of being banned from playgrounds indoor and outdoor. But they might as well be covering their ears and singing "Baby Shark" at the top of their lungs.

Let's just say they don't view my perspective as the Holy Grail they've been looking for.

Those stamping feet and closed fists clearly aren't part of a social media dance craze. And they certainly aren't implying, "I would love to grow in character! Allow me to sit beneath your wise tutelage."

Proverbs 3:1

Still—You've got big (good!) things to say about the heart that seeks wisdom.

Proverbs 6:16, James 4:6

Isaiah 57:15

Proverbs 6:11–12

In reality, proud people are the ones You specifically declare are on Your bad side; You detest arrogance even more than I do. But You extend kindness to the humble. I long for this child to choose Your authority and loving correction most of all.

1 Corinthians 3:6

I can set the table for humility. (Would You show me how, practically speaking?) But really, You're the only One with power to genuinely change this kid's heart and banish the deeply rooted source of the rolled eyeballs. Behavior management aside, I'd love this teachability to come from within.

The heads-up You don't need: This kid is going to want to blame the teacher, the coach, the sibling, and the family ferret rather than accept ownership of their junk or submit to leadership. I ask You not to let their conscience off the hook. Rock-paper-scissors just isn't an option on who's in charge here. Let me demonstrate the art of the respectful plea rather than the slammed door.

Please be relentless in helping this kid look themselves in the eye. Help them assess themselves—strengths, weaknesses, need for instruction, attitude toward the playground monitor—accurately. *Romans 12:3*

Correct elaborate fantasies of their own fabulousness: We don't need a selfie culture here. Though I'd be tempted to settle for someone who admitted to eating the last spoonful of salsa and putting the jar back in the fridge.

Prevent me from shielding my child from healthy guilt and responsibility. Don't let me prize cotton-candy feelings over opportunities to ratchet up their character.

Even when I'm not sure I liked that teacher in the first place. But let's keep that between You and me, shall we?

Amen.

Let Me *Confess* Search Engines Know More *Than I Do*

All-Knowing God,

So the cat may be out of the bag. My child may be onto the idea there are questions I can answer, questions the search engine can answer, and an entire category of questions that are neither.

I may not actually know how many suckers an octopus has or when TV was invented. And I definitely don't know why our friend is sick, or why some very good people are very poor.

I admit a part of me would like to try my hand at bluffing. Surely my poker face is better with people under four feet.

But I am building trust with this kid, whom I do want to ask me questions—so we can be a team of curiosity, thoughtful discussion, and the pursuit of wisdom. Even when "I don't know, but let's find out" is my only recourse. Or I know the answer but would rather be a lot of other places than sitting here answering how poop is made.

Psalm 51:6, Romans 12:3

See, I want to be their go-to person. And I want to learn from my child, too. But that only happens with emotional and intellectual honesty.

Even more than a sermonette to end all sermonettes, You seem to value the relationship and personal ownership from question asking and conversation starting. Let me fan their interest and problem-solving—rather than turn a fire hose on it to quench every possible flame of inquisitiveness. Would You show me how to cultivate that here?

Who knows: Maybe we can look up together how old a tortoise can get. Or wonder out loud about whether Adam and Eve had belly buttons.

So help me be truthful about exactly what I know and what I don't, modeling humility of all kinds—rather than exhaustive to both the topic and the child. Which will probably get me farther than the job title of "Expert in All Kid Queries." You're the only One with perfect knowledge.

Deuteronomy 29:29, 1 John 3:20

Maybe we should start a kid-parent combined list of all we want to ask when we meet You? Although in the awe of being with You in person, I have a strong hunch it will all fade like invisible ink.

amen.

When Grades Fall, *Lord,* Lift Us Up

To the Perfect One,

After seeing the latest grades, I am suppressing the fierce desire to chain my child to their homework. If only D meant my child's performance was simply . . . *Delightful.*

Yet You know my child and all the unique circumstances, or lack thereof, resulting in this grade. So help me ask the right questions, sift through this kid's stockpile of reasons (or excuses?), and fail to succumb to the cop-out of the bad teacher, the track practice, the class hamster with an appetite for math worksheets. Help me get to the true roots of what's going on.

I'm grateful for education and this chance to lean into Your image in this kid. But I get it: Study skills and testing performance may not be where that image lies in every child. (What if, in my disappointment, I miss the way You wired them to shine?) Don't let me make the gift into the god. Grades are admittedly a human construct. (A learning-challenged kid's C can be the equivalent of another kid's A+.) And excellence is so much more than who any of us are on paper.

Ephesians 2:10, Colossians 3:23

I long to teach this kid faithfulness, responsibility, and love for excellence as an offering to You—to do the good works today and in the future You've prepped for them. Someday their perseverance and attention to detail will affect far more than themselves. Lead them to maximize their gifts and further their education in ways that further Your Kingdom.

1 Peter 4:10–11

What's Your will for my child, in this moment and in the future? Would You grant me creative ways to motivate them, in the way they're made, toward Your ends?

On earth, would You have ever gotten a less-than-top grade? Maybe if Your mom needed help during Your study session, or You were exhausted from all-night prayer. What if You were made a solid B student, or worked Your tail off for straight C's?

Yet in Your flawless performance on our behalf, You already delivered the only verdict on our value that truly matters. End of story.

My worth and this child's aren't touched by our abilities or performance. Don't let me confuse Your idea of success with human success. Or importance. Wealth. Approval. Fear of failure and weakness (theirs, mine). In my child's failures, let me sit with them, clearly separating value from achievement—while still calling them to the fullest version of who You've made them to be.

Point me back to how success for this child means them loving You with their life. It has very little to do with SAT scores. Great news, right now.

amen.

For Swimming *Upstream in the* **Media Deluge**

To the One Who Is Wisdom,

Playing Media Evaluator can feel like a minefield: I face my child's stink eye in one corner for saying no (BOOM!). Or their vulnerability when I say yes to media that harm their developing hearts and minds (BOOM!). Or their alienation from peers because I'm the only parent who refused (BOOM!). Or unwittingly setting precedents because I said yes to that thing that was "way worse than this one" (BOOM!).

And frankly, reviewing lyrics of the new band "on *everyone's* playlists" didn't originally make the top of today's priority list.

Once my kids fly the nest, I don't want them clueless about how to evaluate the media everyone's gulping down like Kool-Aid. I also don't want them, like a Christian bubble kid, holing up with their Jesus music and flipping out when someone rolls out a playlist.

Rather than sweeping categories of good and bad, my kids need to understand intricate combinations of good and evil, truth and untruth, and redemptive threads You've hidden in culture, pointing people Your way.

Philippians 4:8

1 John 2:15

But let's just admit media and social media aren't out for my kids' glowing mental health and thriving. And You command us to think on what's true, noble, right, lovely—never to love what the world offers. So much of this stuff is rewiring my kids' brains long before they can truly discern. Help me think bigger than simple rating systems.

Maybe this cringey song or sensory-overload video game is my window to openly converse in biblical-worldview training (versus my kids' "I dunno. My parents said no").

As usual, gently leading my kids toward biblical conclusions is 100 percent more effective than my doing it for them. But can I point out, this takes a lot more uphill work? Some days I wish I could just flip on this virtual babysitter and call it good.

Please give us wisdom to ask the right questions—about core values depicted. About how those desires are met in ways Your Word says are okay, or aren't. About ways modern media and social media overpromise: "Romantic love and the perfect eye cream solved all my problems!"

You're the ultimate yes to the core thirst of every song, every movie, every video game.

Jeremiah 2:13, John 14:4

Build discernment in my kids through constant application of Your Word—from sketchy video games to the music artist I'd rather consign to headphones only.

2 Timothy 3:16–17, Hebrews 5:14

Amen.

Give Us Vision Beyond the Bubble *(and Our Zip Code)*

Culture Author,

You made the world a big, breathtakingly beautiful, diverse place on purpose. If I'm not intentional, my child's life could be vanilla—confined to our tax bracket, our perspectives and ideas, our type of people, our understanding of You.

Shake us up, so we can know, love, and appreciate You more. Without other perspectives, our views of You and Your Word are one-dimensional. We could minimize and flatten the awe You deserve.[19]

If the world is a book, staying with people just like us is like reading only a paragraph. So whether we've got cash to leave our zip code or not, help us choose deep relationships with those different from us. Make us people who listen, who long to know, understand, and love beyond our comfort zone—and who locate Your image in every person, treating them that way because we love You.

Matthew 22:37–39, Mark 10:12

Give us anger for injustice, poverty, and oppression, tears for those suffering, and enough craziness to think we can make a dent.[20]

Amen.

Prayers *for* Joy & Gratitude

Bless This Ice Cream *for Dinner*

Beckoner of Little Children,

There's a lot I need to teach this kid before launch: how to bake cookies, write a check, clean the bathroom, tie a tourniquet.

And I've got high hopes. I mean, Nobel Peace Prize winner, Poet Laureate, full-ride scholarship winner, and memorizer of the entire Bible may not be feasible. But I'm sure we can manage one of those. Right after we teach this kid to consistently wear underwear.

I'm saying that with how much I love this kid and hope for them, perfectionism might become an issue—leaving me to coax and squeeze and scold them right into the failure I'm desperate for them to avoid. (You sure I can't build heaven here?)[21]

But You and I were both kids once. Somewhere under these emails, grocery lists, permission slips, tax returns, and a pile of laundry resembling Denali more every day—remind me what it's like to be my child's age. What it's like to not remember the rules, not know (or care) what's expected, not understand. To feel small and afraid and bored. To wish you could play even when you forgot to make the bed. To feel so much energy pumping through your body it feels impossible to sit still and be polite.

Mark 10:15

Being a child at any age means vulnerability. Helplessness. Dependence. In fact, You require I be like them, bringing nothing except my trust in Your love.

So unwind me for the sake of this child. Help me feed curiosity and desire for fun, creating expectations that call my child up without being graceless or unattainable, with no room for a real-life child and their real-life body, brain, and heart. Let me throw caution to the wind and serve ice cream or not-so-fiber-filled cereal for dinner every now and then, or camp out in a fort in the living room, even though my back may scowl at the consequences.

Whether popping underwear on my head from the laundry, sliding down the stairs on my backside, finger-painting with shaving cream together, or slathering on a jelly mustache and a crazy accent, grant me creativity to pry open wide spaces for childhood. Let my kids dive deep into silliness and delight—and remember me right alongside them in these blindingly short years, before life becomes much more complicated.

Through this kid, remind me what moments or even seasons of freedom look like when it seems to make more sense to hustle, perform, worry, protect, and achieve. And keep us stocked with sprinkles and whipped cream.

amen.

Bring Us *to* Wide-Open Spaces *(on the Calendar)*

Restorer of Souls,

I am tired of being tired. It's like this ragtag little band is a bunch of human *doings* rather than human *beings*.[22] Is it just me, or does this schedule have me on a short leash, rather than the other way around?

Maybe it's a conspiracy! These instructors and coaches and dental hygienists are surely in cahoots so my offspring will do their evil bidding!

Wonderful Counselor, would You grant me clarity? Something tells me You didn't walk the planet burned to a crisp all the time. And I'm afraid I'm setting the pace for my kids' adult lives; heaven forbid this carries to another generation. What are the healthy rhythms of rest and joy You hope we'll receive with open arms?

(I guess being efficient doesn't matter if we're doing the wrong things in the first place.[23])

Remind me what my family hopes to gain from each commitment. But help me, too, to look at our family with accuracy on what we can actually do with joy, still being able to love each other genuinely.

Romans 12:3, 9

I acknowledge that opportunity doesn't automatically equal Your call. Are we buying into some lies about what matters? For the love of Mike, which ones?

They can't do it without me. Can't miss that opportunity. We can't disappoint them. My kids would be left out. Underwater cello lessons are necessary for success.

I can't say no.

What if all these yeses are leading to some unfortunate, even sad, noes?

I'm sorry, the energy to be patient was sapped by the lacrosse match an hour ago. No, playing a board game might just send me over the edge right now. No, we don't have time to talk—grab your cleats. We'll hit the drive-through; why am I the one convincing you nuggets are a good idea?

Let our priorities—I mean *Your* priorities—shape this schedule rather than the other way around. I don't want to check all the boxes just to forget the room to love each other.

1 Corinthians 13:1–3

You remind me doing more isn't the same as living more. When rest descends—maybe between jiujitsu and Mandarin homework for preschoolers—let us discern between what's relaxing, what's rejuvenating, and what's idle. When You present us green pastures and still waters, let us not mow the grass and swim laps.

Amen.

Show Me Your Glory, *Even If It's Just Getting Them to Flush*

Victorious One,

Here's to little wins.

In this home, they might look like celebrating the five-alarm tantrum that finally was not thrown. Or remembering to put their cereal bowl in the dishwasher before the crusty-enough-to-be-chipped-off phase. Or holding back that remarkably witty but not-so-Christlike comeback.

I want to be a parent who—without being condescending—fishes out and celebrates the wins, the progress. Pretty sure You're that kind of Dad.

Ephesians 1:18

So give me eyes to see the good You're creating in these kids—because You complete every good work You start.

Philippians 1:6

Many of Your miracles, rather than splitting the sea or healing a leper, look more like springtime: growth barely visible, yet awe-inspiring and hopeful when I step back. I am confident You are creating life and miracles in my own family, day by day, even moment by moment. I just need to be patient and alert.

It can be hard to know how to react when I'm disappointed. Flip my child's weaknesses over for me, so I can witness the strength You've instilled on the other side. I trust You're writing the story here, in all its crash and burns and hard-won hurrahs. (Or tiny ones.) You choose to see value despite attitudes and rebellion and blindness.

Romans 5:6, 8; Ephesians 2:7

Amidst the back talk, potty accidents, spills of juice on the counter, belching in church, and eyes rolled so hard they might pop out into the overflowing hamper, help me see what these kids are doing right. And recognize it. Even in the middle of all the cringe, I want this child to see Your patience. Your promise. Your hope. Your smile.

So please give me Your discernment with the standards and expectations I hold dear. Show me what hopes are appropriate for this child's story, personality, weaknesses, strengths, and path to You.

I'm not out to champion mediocrity here. I'm about celebrating what You're doing, and what my child participates with You in—showing them Your delight, until someday, we can all party with You together.

Meanwhile, could You teach my immediate reactions to use their inside voice?

amen.

Release Us *from the* Clutches *of the* Dollar Aisle

To the One Who Is Enough for Us,

Remind me for a moment of all the kids' meal toys, broken dollar-store trinkets, and dolls or action figures I have stepped on, refrained from cursing at, and/or schlepped out of our home in the last six months while my kids beg for more eye candy. Free us all from the fickle gremlins of human emotion and desire convincing my kids that this toy will be the one that makes their lives really sing.

From the grocery store to the dot-com, it's like nails on a chalkboard: my kids begging for the next thing, and with every no, a response like I've murdered the class hamster. ("Cleanup for whining on aisle twelve"?)

I long to communicate to my kids that *more stuff* doesn't mean *more and better life.*

Matthew 6:21

But even from my own life, I see that where my heart is, my treasure is. It's not about the money, or that rubber duckie with the pirate eye patch, or the pair of kicks we must have or the apocalypse will be triggered. It's the treasure that the money or possession gets us: the Control. Safety. Praise. Reputation. Acceptance. Comfort. Power. Self-value.

Mark 4:19

You've designed us so the holes in our hearts are never truly filled by more stuff, more food, more activity. Not only that; this stuff chokes Your words in us, edging out our hunger for You like a bag of potato chips before dinner. No tech gadget or doll accessory or wow-worthy app can offer the soul-level satisfaction we're really hungry for—in You, the Bread of Life.

Jeremiah 2:13, John 6:35, Philippians 4:12–13

Not to mention, I hate that so many cheap goods are manufactured in unjust conditions, exploiting other people, even kids. So swivel my eyes away from the bargain-basement sale on things we don't need—we just want.

Redirect not just the loves of my heart but also my child's. Show us how to be captivated by the Giver rather than the gifts. Free my family from the headlock of materialism, pleasure seeking, and anxiety. Even the next toy brick set is just not worth that.

Luke 8:14

You made life's pleasures as good gifts, as wide-open windows for gratitude. I am so grateful we can afford not just what we need but what we enjoy. Swap out our discontentment with thankfulness—and show me how to shuttle my kids' hearts in that direction.

1 Timothy 4:4

And away from that ugly, ugly stuffie.

Amen.

A Prayer *for* Travel Truces *and* Grace *on the Go*

Author of Every Place,

Despite the movements of heaven and earth to get this herd of turtles out the door . . . thank You for the gift of traveling together, the resources for this adventure, and whoever finished off the last of the milk. Before we lock the door, please bring to mind all the stuff we've spaced out on while trying to take this show on the road.

Philippians 2:14

Starting with the little things, bubble up thankfulness in us. Keep us from complaining or arguing (I recognize this is a big ask). Help us appreciate one another and bathe each other in kindness and delight, even when someone is purposefully sliding over the invisible line in the back seat. We could collectively land the golden ticket to Willy Wonka's chocolate factory—but if we don't love each other, this whole trip would be a bust.

1 Corinthians 13:1–3

Would You help me set the tone of graciousness, gratitude, silliness, peace, and fun? The kids in this little circus sideshow need to glimpse Your delight in them through me.

Psalm 149:4, Isaiah 62:4

You and I both know something is going to go wrong. Perhaps royally. But every interruption is from Your hand.

So grant me grace for trust and flexibility with every forgotten toothbrush and every oblivious customer service representative.

When, not if, my kids act in a manner unbecoming—give me presence of mind in the moment to behave like You would. For all our sakes, give me wisdom on what to discipline and what to let slide in this curious role I play as Family Thermostat.

These days with these sticky, pink-cheeked little sweethearts/monsters are short, no matter how long they feel. Create memories in all of us of freewheeling beauty, connection, and togetherness. And whet our appetites for Heaven.

Which presumably will not include, "Why didn't you go before we left?"

Amen.

This Little Light of Mine *(That Didn't Burn Down the Church on Christmas Eve)*

Immanuel,

Something tells me the innovator of the candlelight service didn't have toddlers, preschoolers, or budding pyromaniacs in their family. ("Silent Night" also seems unlikely considering You were 100 percent human?)

While I am dwelling in reality, chances are, our holidays won't be perfect. Between un-wiped-off boots, overweening greed, cabin fever, family pictures with nose-picking-enthralled kids, and discussions of partisan politics, something (anything!) may go awry.

Yet amidst burned turkeys or ice storms, let us welcome the three wise gifts of patience, perspective, and enduring love.

Fill us with belly laughs at mishaps from this messy planet You chose to come all the way into, from diapers to puberty. Overcome us with incomprehensible peace as we trust Your timing, and the Baby who would be hunted as a political enemy and forced into immediate exile. Let hope shine over heart-rending situations.

Isaiah 53:4

I acknowledge some of my family members may not be healthy, well-behaved, attractive, well-spoken, and making wise choices. But You sacrificially loved us and chose weakness, despite ours. In light of the yelling in the car on the way to church: I could use a hand in replicating this.

So let a sense of soul-anchoring joy swallow us whole when happiness evaporates like a sugar high. Let our family's service to each other, even as it demands large chunks of us, be like the aroma of gingerbread and fresh pine to You.

Like a barn-turned-maternity-ward—remake our noise, and what stinks, into that which is breathtaking, throbbing with all-enveloping love. Thank You that You chose to live among the lowly, and people who break everything. Thanks for having a vision bigger than a stable.

Turn every one of our hearts to wisely seek You, even when You feel far away, or the journey demanding. God-with-Us, let Your presence and love sustain us until our next imperfect Christmas.

And help us remember where we kept the batteries and receipts.

amen.

A Call *for* Safety Through *the* Toy Brick Minefield

Giver of All Perfect Gifts,

Could You remind me whether "cleanliness is next to godliness" actually made it into the Bible? Because this abundance of toys in my house is actually sometimes more than I can handle. As in, my cup overflows. What do I have that You didn't give me?

Psalm 23:5

1 Corinthians 4:7

Not only do we have clean water and a (usually) flushing toilet; we've got action figures and dress-up clothes out the wazoo. We've got a floor, even when fully carpeted by toys; clearly I walk by faith, not by sight. We've got access to trash collection, which I am meditating on rather seriously at the moment. And access to medical care. Which I may need after the next toy brick skewering my foot. Mental health services remain available to me; helpful, though I'm fairly certain my sanity is around here somewhere. Maybe under that stuffie with the eye dangling out.

Sometimes Your favor shows up in the form of a vehicle (life-sized or matchbox-sized), or a lovely home, or being able to pry out the doll's head stuck in said toilet. But sometimes it doesn't. Sometimes our prosperity actually stands in between us and the only thing that matters: You.

Matthew 19:16–26

Luke 12:15

Protect my family from the lie that an overflowing life exists in a bunch of stuff. Don't let all . . . *this* . . . snooker us into thinking we're nourished, full, and happy. You're

Philippians 4:12–13, Jeremiah 2:13

enough for this family when we have a lot or don't—and the only One that satisfies.

But standing in toys up to my shins to the point they're a health hazard, I thank You for the "more than enough" of right now. For kids entertained and educated, stimulated and delighted, whose curiosity is fed and nurtured—and, at times, gratuitous enough it can be dropped on the floor.

Meanwhile, keep me from overfunctioning when my kids should be on cleanup here in Area 51—whether to make me feel like a better parent, prevent future migraines, cause potential guests to think better of a family otherwise residing in squalor, or serve my kids. Let me empower, not enable or entitle.

Thank You, thank You for too much stuff. Your character is to give so much more than we need, so we can be generous in every way. Remind us to share our gifts. (Maybe some of those toy bricks?)

2 Corinthians 9:8–11

Now, if only that plastic wand over there—if I could get to it—could whisk this all away into organized toy bins. *Expeloramus hurricanus juvenilicas.*

Amen.

Lord, *Help Us* Put On Party Hats

Faithful One,

Philippians 1:6

I think I just witnessed success! Much gratitude for letting me glimpse You at work here, continuing to complete what You started. Every good thing is from You; there's nothing we have that isn't.

1 Corinthians 4:7, James 1:17

So I'm taking this little moment to celebrate with You.

You know all about how this little flare of character—or this little glimpse into how You've uniquely gifted my child for the future You've planned—is perhaps hard-won. It's meaningful to me right now, and You see why. (Thank You for understanding and knowing me so intimately.)

Genesis 16:13

You're the "God who Sees" all the obscure moments of parenting: the child finally peeing where they're supposed to. Or overlooking the slight from the sibling. Or the mumbled "thanks" for the ride. Or finally (finally!) hanging up the towel.

You run out to the prodigal, calling for a ring, a robe, and a party. I wanna be like this: the parent who celebrates any way kids "come home" or just choose what's good and holy.

Luke 15:11–32

You've witnessed me helping with homework, or fishing poop out of the tub, or doing the dinner dishes, the daily finish line so close I can smell it. So You, more than anyone, really *get* how much the wins mean. You serve up mercies tailor-made for each day.

Lamentations 3:22–23

Grant me Your eyes to see more of Your glory in this circus, even when others might not consider it worth buying a ticket. *Exodus 33:18*

When things are lookin' grim, remind me of moments like these—and help me mine the nuggets of Your faithfulness there, too.

You're always working, whether I see it or not. *John 5:17* Help me be on the lookout for You, and acknowledge You there, not unlike the way You acknowledge and appreciate my out-of-the-spotlight work.

Thanks for celebrating with me—maybe toasting with a cup of apple juice—and for all Your daily faithfulnesses to me and this kid to bring us here to a victory lap, however tiny.

Here's to kids who put dishes in the dishwasher and don't smart off . . . someday.

Amen.

Transform *Our* Whines *into* Worship

Joy Giver,

Confession: I think I could have this kid at a theme park with their best friend, complete with funnel cake, balloon animal, souvenir superhero cape, and slushy, and perhaps the most appropriate T-shirt to purchase would still read, I'D RATHER BE WHINING.

Nixing the complaints is a good discipline for any of us, I know. But please *replace* our complaining. Keep Your praise always on our lips. Our trust constant even when we bomb the spelling test, get bubble gum in our hair, fall in a snowdrift, and throw up in P.E. all on the same day.

Psalm 34:1, Matthew 6:22

Open our eyes to Your beauty and kindness, the gifts You're stacking around us. Even on days that, if every day is a gift, feel more like getting underwear from Grandma.

Keep our brains and conversation from hanging out in blame, punishment, dissatisfaction, anger, or bitterness. Steer us to marinate in what's true, pure, lovely, and admirable everywhere. Including days when the froyo place is out of gummy bears.

Philippians 4:8–9

In the very moment of the whining windup, let me shift my child's focus off circumstances and the 24/7 factory of their desires and expectations. Without being plasticky and fake, let me point them toward how big You are and how You listen to our needs.

Your beef with the grumbly Israelites in the wilderness (do I envision my child, arms crossed?) wasn't about a mom in the desert wanting water for her baby; Hagar did that. It's not wrong to want food in the desert; Jesus did that. It's not wrong, even, to wonder how You're going to accomplish something; David, Mary, and a whole lotta other people did it.

Genesis 16

Matthew 4:2

Psalm 86, Luke 1:34–37

You're not looking for denial, or lack of frustration and disappointment. It's how we handle it, right? You seem to take issue more with entitlement, with a side of unbelief.

So keep me from fueling the complain-train by wheedling, scooping this child into my arms, turning into their cruise director, or, far worse, handing them what they want. Let me reinforce self-control, self-soothing, patience, and plain ol' contentment.

Would You hand me practical ideas to kindle gratitude as a culture in this house? Help me recognize the hard work of the janitor. Write the thank-you notes. Name fifty thankful things before we get to soccer.

But most of all, to thank You. (As a toilet-scrubbing parent, I empathize with kindnesses unseen.)

amen.

Lead Us *to* **Gratitude** *for* **Green** *(Not Greener)* **Pastures**

Good Shepherd,

The comparison factor is real—the perfect shoes, the social media following, the contents of the sack lunch, the spring break vacay. Seems like my child loves to strategically compare their outtakes to someone else's highlight reel. Or vice versa, depending on what point they're proving.

At times, social comparison can certainly challenge us toward wisdom, courage, love. It can challenge us to trust You more.

2 Corinthians 12:9–10, Philippians 4:13

But if we're not careful, it can just make us more afraid. It can rob us of joy, contentment, gratitude—swapping it for entitlement, judginess, and an insistence Your gifts aren't enough.

♡ Matthew 6:21

I know that where this kid's heart is, their treasure is. Help me understand: Underneath the quest for the "perfect" body or being invited to the "right" party, what's the prize they crave?

I'm talking the lie they're angling toward, convincing them it'd make life complete. Maybe it's comfort, approval, superiority, status, power, control, or simply a sense of being worthy, *if only*.

We both know the percentage of these that will satisfy my child's soul: exactly zero. You have made us for Yourself, and our hearts are restless until they rest in You. *Jeremiah 2:13*

Somehow, help me receive what's legit about my child's concern—we all want to be liked, not scorned; successful, not failing. But show me how to un-praise the false promises causing this kid to chase the wind. *Ecclesiastes 1:14*

Let us set You before our eyes, and worship You—rather than grades, basketball prowess, awards, or faces around the lunch table. Unchain my child from the endless, anxious toil of the comparison treadmill and the next inane social media trend. (Mind pointing out ways I'm making things worse?) *Psalm 127:1–2, Luke 8:14*

Overrun us with appreciation in a world You stuffed with differences. Someone will always work harder, have more, look better, do better, right? And that's just fine. We don't need to be equally good at everything to be made *on purpose*, for a future only You see. (Palm trees and pine trees are both beautiful and perfect for their climates—but would flounder elsewhere.) Let us lean into Your image. Not someone else's.

You're the best. (Really.)

amen.

Thank You *for a* Love More Overflowing *Than the* Laundry

Lover of Our Souls,

Who would have thought I could love this little person this much?

It's crazy, too, the sheer volume of affection I felt before this child was able to do a thing for me (in fact, I was the one *doing*) other than simply *be themselves.*

(Is this how You feel about me?)

Thank You for every way I glimpse Your glory in a smorgasbord of goodnesses in this kid. Thank You for the joy I feel just being with them and near them, for getting a front seat to watch them grow and giggle, learn and light up, mature and make wiser decisions.

Joshua 4:1–9

Your people set up stone monuments to never forget what You'd done for them. Show me how to somehow commemorate my gratitude for Your faithfulness, Your over-the-top kindness to me in the form of a child. (And maybe help me remember this the next time they leave dirty underwear precisely nine inches from the hamper.)

Psalm 127:3–5

I agree with You—plus some backflips and fireworks—that this child is a gift. Show me how to manage this privilege in a way that brings You deep pleasure.

Help me lean into trusting You while my feelings are high. Remind me how perfect Your gift is on future forehead-smacking days when I don't feel this sure.

I may not always feel all these big feels. So show me how to convey my affection for this kid in the ups and also downs that inevitably pop up in a parent's life. And keep us always finding ways to appreciate each other, just being present in whatever moments we're given together.

Thanks for loving us both, even more than the glow I feel right now. I may be glowing more with parenting perspiration next week—but for now, I simply thank You.

Ephesians 3:17–19

Amen.

A Plea *to* Make Time Go *as* Slowly *as* This Kid Doing Chores

To the One Who Holds Our Days,

Eighteen summers. That's all I get.

Seems like yesterday I was trying to wade out of a sea of diapers, hoping to brush my teeth once in forty-eight hours. All that stuff about the days being long and the years being short? It didn't feel as true when I was stumbling around, twenty-three minutes of a REM cycle to my name.

But this kid is growing up.

Psalm 139:1–6, 13–16; Ephesians 2:10

Somehow when I look at them, I see all the versions: the kid falling on their bottom after a few drunken-sailor-style steps. The one in the bathtub making a beard out of bubbles (or just pooping in the tub). The one bouncing up and down in an attempt to dance for the first time. And the child before me, like an instant photo developing definition and color according to Your plan.

Makes my heart hurt, even as it blooms.

Who knew—when I was just making sure this kid was wearing clean underwear—that loving so much could sting like this? Or that the health and goodness of a child growing could feel like my heart being wedged from my body with a spoon?

So on the days I'd rather be scrolling social media, or streaming in bed with a pint of ice cream in hand: Let me set aside what's distracting to be all here, in these moments dripping through my hands. Open my eyes for the beauty and goodness tucked in the everyday slices of time—whether running to the grocery store together, stirring a batch of pancake batter, sharing a great movie, staring down a sunset, chasing a ball.

Psalm 92:2, 128:24, 1 Thessalonians 5:18

Help me seize Your opportunities to infuse these days with substance. Intention. Expressing my boatloads of affection for this knucklehead. And worshipping You the whole way. Thank You, Lord, for this child, Your idea.

1 Samuel 1:27, Psalm 127:3, James 1:17

And if You could slow time down, even more than it takes this kid to put away a laundry basket of clothes? Bonus.

Amen.

Our Father, *Who Art in* Parks

To the Author of Fun,

Psalm 104:25–26

From squirrels to dolphins, otters to tiger cubs, puppies to chimps, You get a kick out of handcrafting creatures that play. You are the God of belly laughs, handstands, and farting. If I love watching my kids have a good time this much, I gotta imagine You perfect that art.

Thank You that I live in a place valuing kids enough that communities invest in them. Kids are helpless, status-less, powerless, résumé-less, dependent, trusting. They don't reserve affection; they are undignified. They bring very little to the table, other than the fact they are ours. (And kinda cute. Most of the time.)

Yet You require that we contributing members of society become like them.

Matthew 18:3

So thanks for the opportunity for this kid to develop some physical ability, relationships, imagination, confidence, and that sense of "I can."

Please keep this time carefree and safe from everything from splinters to bullies to tag played right smack in front of the swing set. Kindle my kids' curiosity, brains, motor and social skills, resilience, competence, and healing through Your great idea of play.

And let them resist temptation to throw rocks and tantrums, or pee outside five feet from a restroom.

Amen.

Prayers *for* Physical & Emotional Strength

Now I Lay Me Down to Sleep *(Please Stay Out Cold till the Alarm Beeps)*

God of Rest,

Nothing quite rockets the adrenaline like a child's yell piercing one's REM cycle. Hard to say whether I'd like a good night's sleep more for this kid or to deliver myself from a sense of consciousness resembling scrambled eggs.

Neither of us is the holiest version of ourselves without sleep. I may be a little desperate.

But even more than some blessed shut-eye, I covet Your wisdom: What's beneath this kid's insomnia?

Help me peer behind the (aggravating, exhausting) symptoms—whether strictly physical, or more deeply seated. Give me the patience to be present, to engage, to ask. Despite that, I would rather be dreaming about a beach in Jamaica. Or just dreaming, period.

Grant me insight, especially if my child's experiencing anxiety. Fear is so much more than monsters under the bed. It's tied to who we are and what we worship. Maybe we fear loss of control. Being vulnerable. Others' opinions. Whether we can trust others—and trust that You never let us fall. You free us from the terror of night.

Psalm 55:22

Psalm 91:5

In my brain fog, grant presence of mind to usher my child's anxieties to You in prayer together. Because You care for us, even when I can hardly remember my name. May Your peace, beyond understanding, guard this child's heart and mind.

Philippians 4:6–7, 1 Peter 5:7

It's You who welcome the weary (and bleary-eyed), who offer rest to our souls with gentleness and humility. My child's fears are a chance to bathe a developing brain in God realities stronger than fear, in You as our mutual source of value, safety, and peace. Help my child intentionally capture every thought that's not from You and make it obedient to You.

Matthew 11:28–30

Psalm 4:8

* *2 Timothy 1:7, 2 Corinthians 10:5*

Still, I ask for the discernment on when and how to show this child what Your comfort, care, and closeness look like in the middle of the night, and when to build their ability to self-soothe.

Give me holy creativity, so both of us can settle into the rhythms You created for our bodies. Restore our souls, and keep us both absolutely unmoving until morning.

Amen.

For When *My Child* Sneezes Directly *in* My Face

Great Physician,

The plague of one sort or another has descended. I'm grateful that, in defiance of sin's destruction in this world, You granted my child an immune system. Fire up that baby, as well as my own. Which is feeling increasingly relevant.

Please protect us from the nasties we can see, and those we can't. (Thanks for the untold ways You already have—and every one of my child's healthy days.) Don't let this thing topple my family like a row of dominoes. I beg for Your holy firewall.

I ask that this sickness would be a blissful nonevent that we have the privilege of barely remembering. In the weakness and vulnerability of my child's body, show me moments to surround them with compassion and nurture, whether in the form of cartoons, Popsicles, picture books, snuggling, time off, quiet songs, vaporizers, or even changing the bedsheets.

Psalm 34:18, 147:3; Isaiah 61:1; Matthew 9:36

For this pink-cheeked kid in the cute pajamas, let me sketch the picture of how You love us. You lean toward us in our weakness.

Please give patience amidst crankiness, wisdom amidst whining, serenity in sleepless nights, perseverance in laundry, grace when barfed upon.

I pray for parents and kids for whom a healthy childhood isn't the norm.

Thank You for Your gift of science and intelligent, dignified health care—for every person squinting over a microscope, squirreled away in a research lab, writing grant letters, or poring through medical journals so my child can frolic through life with less danger, more dancing. Grant wisdom, discernment, and kindness to every health professional who serves us. Please give all of us awareness, resources, and proactivity to know when and how to seek help on my child's behalf, including long-term solutions.

I ask that all who toss their cookies would make it to the toilet with the lid open.

Amen.

Bring Us *from* Waiting Room *to* Sticker Reward

True Healer,

Confession: Medical and dental appointments may not be my favorite part of parenting. I might rather be, I don't know . . . scrubbing the toilet or fish tank.

Perhaps as a consequence of my crazy levels of love for this kid, turns out this whole "convince my child to do what might sting" isn't my jam. But I know my desire to protect them from pain is an expression of Your own fierce protection. For all of their cool outfits, superheroes have nothing on You.

Romans 5:3–5, 8:28; James 1:2–4

If I've got such a bigger, more complex perspective than this kid on what they need, remind me of this when You allow stuff that hurts. Even when my limited understanding of the world can't comprehend the thought. You don't dole out pain just for kicks, either. Even You press through pain for long-game rewards that are worth it, hands down.

Romans 8:22–23, Philippians 2:5–11, Hebrews 12:3

In Your wisdom, You made us embodied souls. You honored our bodies—prone to breaking and vulnerability, requiring intimate care by self and community—by taking on one of Your own. The kind of tender, careful nurture and prevention in appointments like these show the world how You care for us. Give me ideas to make this as fun and kid-friendly as possible. Even when it means letting the kid wear a firefighter costume backwards.

John 1:14

Ezekiel 4:14–15, Ephesians 5:29–30

Thank You for all the gifts of science that I enjoy today—plus the ability to afford them, and every second of good health this kid enjoys. Even tiny pinpricks shield my child from diseases, tragedy, and pain they need never witness. A lot of kids around the world wish for the services requiring me to drag this wailing, moaning child through the doctor's office door.

Maybe I'm muscling past old, hairy fears or shame in order to do what's wholesome and best for this kid. Maybe You're using it to shape me, too, just as You've used it to shape me in the past. This child keeps pulling me to a new level of turning to You with deep-seated cares. You were sovereign and loving then, and You will be for a new generation.

Deuteronomy 7:9, Psalm 119:90

So I ask You for peace and age-appropriate maturity for both of us. Please give compassion, wisdom, and thoughtful questions for the professionals caring for my child, as well as for any needed decisions. Send us people to help us who are worthy of this kid's growing trust (and mine). Help me model healthy ways of dealing with fear and vulnerability—in honesty. Bravery. Acceptance. Faith. And maybe celebrating with a sticker or healthy-ish lollipop when we make it through.

Amen.

Heal *Our* Skinned Knees *and* Bruised Egos

Holy Comforter,

I've come to know firsthand why colorful bandages, school nurses, ice packs shaped like animals, and bicycle helmets are childhood staples. These growing, vulnerable little bodies come with such a propensity to bleed, get banged up, and end up on their backsides.

And You've stitched our hearts right to them, tumbling, oozing, bruising. Every now and then we have a day that feels like we landed smack in the bushes, wheels spinning in the air, the rest of us discombobulated and tender.

So I pray for this child and their wounds—those I can and cannot see or kiss or cradle. I pray that for every literal and metaphorical fall You allow throughout life, You will speak Your compassion, perfect purpose, and resurrection over their hurt. You made both of us to do hard things.

Exodus 15:26, Psalms 147:3

You heal the brokenhearted and bind up their wounds; You are the One who heals us. It's who You are. You even went so far as to take our wounds on Your own body.

Psalm 30:2

1 Peter 2:24

In the goose egg after tripping down the stairs, the cast during basketball season (admittedly after the gutsy, questionable attempted skateboarding move), or the breakup with the person my teen was sure was "the one"—somehow let me show the answer to *How does God respond to my pain?*

So empower my resolve to swallow all I-told-you-so's and revisiting of embarrassment in ways that don't repair or reenvision. Let's include any and all observations along the lines of "That was really courageous and dumb," "How's that working for you?" and "Shoulda watched where you're going!" At least until a more appropriate manner and time, if any. Remind me that pain is its own effective tutor, though shame is not.

Give me words and actions of gentleness, resilience, grace, comfort, and vision for a future when we climb back on the banana seat. Shape us both into people who don't lose heart. You offer such sweeping promises to those who overcome.

2 Corinthians 4:16–18, Galatians 6:9

Surely that includes seeing the highest stair one can jump off without breaking open one's forehead, right?

Revelation 2:7, 11, 17, 26–28; 3:5, 12, 21

amen.

When Cartoon Bandages *Don't Cut It*

Man of Sorrows,

Ah, this cuts deep.

It's a wound I can't physically kiss, salve, or disinfect. And the tears last a lot longer than a bad encounter with monkey bars. (I'd take a bike-into-the-bushes collision any day compared with this.)

Just because we can't pull out the butterfly bandages doesn't mean the wounds aren't just as real, if not more so. And much longer lasting.

Psalm 34:18

I think of what I'd do if this kid accidentally ate some turf: I'd hold them, like You hold me when I'm brokenhearted and spirit-crushed. I'd help wash away potentially infectious foreign bodies—maybe like the unhealthy conclusions we could draw about You, or poisonous ways others have acted or spoken. (Might have to rinse and repeat a few days later.) I'd protect the wound, like You do.

Psalm 147:3

In Your parable of the Good Samaritan, I see You as the Samaritan. You see us world-beaten and bleeding, and You tend to our most painful parts. You carry us.

Luke 10:25–37

So as this child encounters this planet's profound pain and its mysteries—perhaps for the first time in a way this personal—show me how to embody Your compassion, and the healing presence that was so much of what You came for. *Isaiah 61:1*

Let me receive this child's tough questions and even anger with the openness, peace, curiosity, and dignity with which You receive mine. In this lifetime, they'll only be the beginning. *Job 3:11, 9:2, 14:14; Habakkuk 11:2; Matthew 11:2–6*

Show me how to point to truth without platitudes. Help me pray with my child, inviting You into our grief even when my thoughts resemble mashed potatoes. You know sadness; You volunteered to carry ours. *Isaiah 53:3–4, John 11:35–36*
You know we are dust. *★Psalm 103:14*

Meanwhile . . . could I ask for You to be present with me, too, so I can even come close to showing my child what Your face looks like when they're hurting? Please hold my own questions, and my own tears in Your bottle. *Psalm 56:8* Thanks for being You even when I don't know which way is up. *2 Timothy 2:13*

I'm grateful You heal both our skinned knees and broken hearts.

amen.

Guard Me *from Bursting Into* Untimely Laughter

God of Impeccable Timing,

Whether this child needs some guidance so they no longer poop in the closet and blame their sibling, or they just slathered their aunt's high-end lipstick on the dog, I am occasionally tempted to laugh out loud at the absurdity of my life.

Ecclesiastes 3:4

But I recognize there's a "time to laugh." And this probably isn't one of them.

You know, too, those times when my child is telling me something highly serious or sensitive but accidentally calls something a swear word. My own willpower *(Do. Not. Laugh.)* often comes up short.

Romans 15:7

In fairness, I imagine that You, as Creator of laughter, witness no small amount of embarrassing human behavior at any given time of day. Yet You welcome us as we are, and ask us to welcome our kids that way.

Far be it from me that my child feels laughed at, rather than safe, in their vulnerability and emotion. Or that a fit of the giggles hamstrings my own discipline.

Hand me words and reactions appropriate to the occasion, rather than my open guffaw at what this kid accidentally just called my mother-in-law.

Proverbs 25:11, Ephesians 4:29

Amen.

For *Whatever the* Day Brings

Perfect Author of This Day,

Psalm 118:24, 139:7–12, 16

You wrote today before time began. *Thank You.*
I can't go anywhere You won't be.

Grant my kids and me the gift of doing this day with You—of walking in lockstep with You and gathering everything we need from You.

Psalm 27:4, John 15:5–7, Galatians 5:25

Whatever happens, whatever "interruptions" and chaos, and wherever these squirrelly kids and I find ourselves at tuck-in time, fill us up with genuine gratitude and admiration for who You are and what You do. Keep our eyes peeled for You.

Satisfy my whole family at soul level—rather than half-baked substitutes from what we do. Or have. Or what people think. Your crazy-loved kids: That's us. Keep our hold on that no matter what.

I reject fear, my inch-deep understanding, and self-salvation in favor of Your perfect love, wisdom, Word, works, and ways. Help me truly know and love You. Teach me how to love these kids—Your kids—and anyone else You put in my path.

Bring it on.

Amen.

Anytime Verses *of* Peace *for* Parents

If any of you lacks wisdom, let him ask God, who gives generously to all without reproach, and it will be given him.
—*James 1:5*

Do not be anxious about anything, but in everything by prayer and supplication with thanksgiving let your requests be made known to God. And the peace of God, which surpasses all understanding, will guard your hearts and your minds in Christ Jesus.
—*Philippians 4:6–7*

Trust in the Lord with all your heart, and do not lean on your own understanding. In all your ways acknowledge him, and he will make straight your paths.
—*Proverbs 3:5–6*

You keep him in perfect peace whose mind is stayed on You, because he trusts in You. Trust in the Lord forever, for the Lord God is an everlasting rock.
—*Isaiah 26:3–4*

"But seek first the kingdom of God and his righteousness, and all these things will be added to you. Therefore do not be anxious about tomorrow. . . . Ask, and it will be given to you; seek, and you will find; knock, and it will be opened to you.
—*Matthew 6:33–34a, 7:7*

Notes

1. Ken Sande, "Relational Peacemaking: Turning Conflict into an Opportunity," *Relational Wisdom 360*, June 2023, https://rw360.org/wp-content/uploads/2023/06/RW_RelationalPeacemaking_StudyGuide.pdf, 4.
2. Sande, "Relational Peacemaking."
3. Brad Hambrick, "Angry Enough to Turn Tables? It Might Not Be Righteous Zeal," *Christianity Today*, August 20, 2024, https://www.christianitytoday.com/2024/08/anger-management-counseling-therapy-psalms.
4. "St. Francis of Assisi: Make me an instrument of your peace," *Archdiocese of Saint Paul & Minneapolis*, accessed December 17, 2024, https://www.archspm.org/faith-and-discipleship/prayer/catholic-prayers/st-francis-of-assisi-make-me-an-instrument-of-your-peace.
5. Elizabeth Stone, *Goodreads*, accessed December 17, 2024, https://www.goodreads.com/quotes/14913-making-the-decision-to-have-a-child---it-is.
6. Jan Johnson, *When the Soul Listens: Finding Rest and Direction in Contemplative Prayer* (Carol Stream, Illinois: Navpress, 2017).
7. R. C. Sproul, *Chosen By God: Know God's Perfect Plan for His Glory and His Children* (Carol Stream, Illinois: Tyndale House Publishers, Inc., 1994), 26.
8. Haesue Jo, "Personal Boundaries Explained—Setting the Emotional Boundaries You Need," *Better Help*, accessed December 17, 2024, https://www.youtube.com/watch?v=y-kqr4A5gog.
9. Andy Crouch, *The Tech-Wise Family: Everyday Steps for Putting Technology in Its Proper Place* (Ada, Michigan: Baker Books, 2017).
10. Tony Reinke, "Six Ways Your Phone Is Changing You," *Desiring God*, July 19, 2014, https://www.desiringgod.org/articles/six-ways-your-phone-is-changing-you.
11. Andy Crouch, *The Tech-Wise Family*.
12. Andy Crouch, *The Tech-Wise Family*.

13. Andy Crouch, *The Tech-Wise Family*.
14. John Piper, "Why Not to Check Your Phone in the Morning," *Desiring God*, July 9, 2015, https://www.desiringgod.org/interviews/why-not-to-check-your-phone-in-the-morning.
15. Jackie Hill Perry, *Upon Waking* (Brentwood, Tennessee: B & H Publishing Group, 2023), 7–8.
16. Mighty Pursuit Podcast, Episode 9, Dr. Arianna Brandolini, April 24, 2024, https://podcasts.apple.com/us/podcast/episode-9-harvard-trained-psychologist-dr-arianna-brandolini/id1731757202?i=1000653392896.
17. Bonnie Kristian, "Train Up a Village," *Christianity Today*, November 14, 2024, https://www.christianitytoday.com/2024/11/kristian-parenting-church-train-up-village.
18. Rob Flood, "The 'Forgotten' Part of Discipline," *FamilyLife*, accessed December 17, 2024, https://www.familylife.com/articles/topics/parenting/parenting-challenges/discipline/the-forgotten-part-of-discipline.
19. *Themelios* 41, no. 3 (January 5, 2017).
20. "A Franciscan Prayer: May God Bless You with Discomfort," *The Paulist Center*, accessed December 17, 2024, https://www.paulistcenter.org/a-franciscan-prayer-may-god-bless-you-with-discomfort.
21. Stephen Witmer, "Parents, You Can't Build Heaven Here," *Desiring God*, October 28, 2015, https://www.desiringgod.org/articles/parents-you-cant-build-heaven-here?utm_medium=feed&utm_source=feedpress.me&utm_campaign=Feed%3A+dg-articles.
22. Peter Scazzero, *Emotionally Healthy Spirituality: Unleash a Revolution in Your Life in Christ* (Grand Rapids, Michigan: Zondervan, 2017).
23. Matt Perman, *What's Best Next: How the Gospel Transforms the Way You Get Things Done* (Grand Rapids, Michigan: Zondervan, 2014), 49.

Index

About *the* Author

Janel Breitenstein, also known as The Awkward Mom, shares gospel-centered parenting insights forged from raising four spirited children. Trained as a conflict coach through Peacemaker Ministries (now Relational Wisdom 365), she's passionate about helping families navigate struggles, applying God's grace and wisdom.

Janel began her career with NavPress, contributing to *The Message Bible*, before transitioning to FamilyLife Publishing. Her practical, authentic writing on topics like marriage and parenting (especially navigating tough discussions with kids) has reached millions through her books, blog, and publications like *Focus on the Family* and *Christianity Today*. Janel also speaks at women's retreats and conferences, inspiring others to embrace vulnerability in their relationships with God and family.

For five years, Janel and her husband served in Uganda with Engineering Ministries International (eMi), supporting poverty relief and development through structural design and construction management for Christian organizations. Now living in Colorado, Janel faces the joys and challenges of parenting teens—snark, hormones, and all—while equipping others to build emotionally healthy relationships at every stage of life. She engages in meaningful conversations on faith, family, and parenting at JanelBreitenstein.com.